When life feels messy

Daily inspiration for soothing the soul and calming the heart

Kartya Wunderle

ISBN 978-0-9922734-3-9
Written by Kartya Wunderle
Compiled by Nola Wunderle
Edited by All Smiles Creative
Cover Artwork & Layout Design by Novu Creative

Printing

Lightning Source | Ingram (USA/UK/EUROPE/AUS)

Published by Phoenix Rising Press
nwunderle@bigpond.com

 A catalogue record for this book is available from the National Library of Australia

© Kartya Wunderle 2018

© 2018. This publication is copyright. Other than for the purposes of and subject to the conditions prescribed under the Copyright Act, no part of it may in any form or by any means (electronic, mechanical, micro copying, photocopying, recording or otherwise) be reproduced, stored in a retrieval system or transmitted without prior written permission. Enquiries should be addressed to the owner Kartya Wunderle.

Contents

Introduction VII
Change 1
Courage 12
Determination 29
Faith 40
Forgiveness 73
Gratitude 78
Life 92
Love 191
Positivity 209

I dedicate this book to my children
Bella and Ethan.

Introduction

To gain a true and genuine perspective, use your heart to look at reality; use your intuition to find the truth, and harness love to block yourself from any negativity that is directed towards you. There is no higher form of protection than love, so fill your heart with compassion and send it out to all you come across – regardless of what's been said or done in the past. It takes strength, not weakness, to forgive others, so forgive often and forgive generously, knowing that it will make you stronger and more at peace in the long-term. Give love simply and easily – not because you want or expect it in return but because love is truly healing. Compared to hatred, love is easy. Hatred is harder to do, takes much more energy and it hurts. And whatever you direct at others, you'll receive back tenfold – so think carefully about what you want to put out into the Universe. In love you are healed. In hatred you are not. So what will you choose? ♥

Change

When life feels messy

Once you let go of your perceived limitations, you allow yourself to realise your potential.

– –

Nothing ever stays the same. Change is always happening. Embrace the change in your life and go with the flow. Recognise that change is a beautiful thing.

– –

As soon as you let go of the idea that your life will magically fix itself, the sooner you can accept that it is you who has to be the one to change things for yourself. You hold all the power within to create the life you want; no one else can do it for you.

– –

Change

As soon as you let go and embrace the change within and around you, something more wonderful will come along and your whole life will change for the better.

– –

Walk away from the things that weigh you down. It's not worth the heartache to hold on to them.

– –

Sometimes you need to throw away pieces of your past in order to free up space so that you can move forwards. Try throwing something away each day or each week. As time moves on and you throw away old emotions and pieces of your past, your sense of freedom will increase.

– –

When life feels messy

Surrender all your pain, anger, blame and sadness to the light. Let yourself be free so that you can start your journey of healing and self-love. There's no need to hold on to negative emotions anymore; it's time to let go of them and find your true path.

– –

Sometimes we forget to see what we've got, and instead focus on what we don't have. When you do this, you leave yourself feeling empty or wishing for more. Instead, you should turn your attention to the things you already have in your life, and be grateful for them. Changing your thoughts can change your life.

– –

Change

If you want to change your future, start by being kind and compassionate to everyone you meet. Let go of judgement and anger and see the world with open eyes. There are underlying reasons for everyone's behaviour and actions, so be understanding and tolerant. Think before you speak and look for the lessons. If the same situation keeps arising, this is a lesson you must recognise and learn. Once you do, you'll find it hard to repeat it in the future. To change your world, you must first start with you.

– –

The world is always changing, people are always changing, nature is always changing, relationships always change, and change is always changing. Change is a beautiful thing; it moves you forward and propels you to new beginnings and magical places.

– –

When life feels messy

Flow with the change that's happening within. Let the transformation take hold so that you can fly. Don't try to resist it, don't fight it, just go with it. You are awakening and being born again. Let it happen, shed the old layers of your former self and begin to be who you were meant to be.

– –

You can't keep complaining about your life unless you are willing to take the steps to fix it. You are the one in control; you can go to numerous people for advice but unless you're willing to listen and act, then stop complaining. Take back your power and take charge of your life. Be the one to rise up to the challenge instead of letting it get the better of you. You can do anything you choose to do if you give it a try.

– –

Change

One foot in front of the other, that's all it takes to make a change. Don't worry about how fast or slow you're going as long as you don't stop. Don't be frightened of the changes, changes are for your greater good, so welcome them and embrace them like a friend, and let these changes transform you into who you are meant to be.
– –

When life feels messy

You are blossoming, you are changing, even if you can't see it yet, know that you are. Just by being here and reading these affirmations, you are emerging, you are emerging; you are allowing yourself to awaken to the divine that resides within you. You're opening your awareness to all that surrounds you, you're starting to see the underlying reason for everything and for everyone you meet, you are empowering yourself to see beyond the illusions that have been placed upon you by others. You are allowing yourself to see that you are connected to all things surrounding you. You are awakening and evolving all at once; enjoy every moment of your newfound path. Be proud of yourself for coming this far and sticking with it.

– –

Change

Do not fear the changes taking place inside of you. Always remember that changes happen every day and it is up to us to embrace them. The seasons change, caterpillars change, puppies change, we as humans change, and life changes all the time. Don't let it be a challenge in your mind, instead let go and allow it to happen because many wonderful and magical things happen when we allow it. And if you have no direction while your changes are taking place, do not become disillusioned, instead stop for a moment and go inside yourself, for inside of YOU and all of your being is where you will find your direction.

– –

When life feels messy

Every day of your life is constantly changing; we learn something from living and being aware in each moment. So take the time today to reflect on where you were two years ago, and then see where you are now. It's a massive change. What have you learned? How far are you on your path? It's a beautiful time to take a look back and see the changes that have been made to propel you forwards. If you don't feel like you've progressed then just trust that you have; otherwise you wouldn't be here right now reading these words.

– –

Change

We all have to learn to accept things the way they are. As much as we try to control situations, sometimes control can exacerbate the very problems we are battling in our minds. Look at yourself and ask "is it me or is it them?" And if it's them, then you need to accept the way they are, and you need to find a way of dealing with the situation. Once you accept the situation, life will feel a lot less complicated and this will enable you to find peace with the situation and within yourself.

– –

Courage

Courage

Fears are merely negative thoughts that you have created in your mind.

- -

Free yourself from the walls you have built upon yourself and find the help you need to get through your problems. Sometimes we can be stuck so far behind our own walls that we are unable to see a way of getting out. You deserve all the help and support you need, so reach out to someone today – a friend or even a stranger. It may be just what you need to save you. We are all one, and we all have battles to fight; coming together can help in more ways than you can imagine. Don't fight alone; there is always someone who can help you.

- -

When life feels messy

You can't start living the life of your dreams if you are still doing the same thing. Be different, step outside your comfort zone, dare to dream, and do what you thought impossible. Pushing yourself beyond your own limits gets easier every time you do it, and it will change your life.

– –

Be your own unique self. Do not conform to what others think you should be. Follow your own path, follow your own rules and let yourself shine the way you want. People will love you for who you are and if they don't, then walk away. You deserve to be around people who will appreciate you for being you.

– –

Courage

Think about the goals and dreams that you have for your one precious life. Now imagine that you can achieve those dreams. Imagine walking out into the world, with no fear in your mind and your head empty of doubt. This is what your imagination was like when you were a child; when your potential was limitless. Think now about your life and your goals. You can achieve them. You just need to step out and create what you came here to do. Don't hold yourself back by fear or perceived limitations. You can create whatever it is you dream of. It's only fear that is holding you back, so fly free and create the life you really want to be living.

– –

When life feels messy

Hiding behind doors won't take you to all the magical places you need to visit. Take a chance, open your eyes, be brave and look at everything with new, childlike wonder. To change your life, you need to see and experience things you've never seen or experienced before. Now is the time to learn all that you can, for your new adventure.

– –

Healing begins once you find the courage to take the steps you need. You may find that between each step there are things you don't like but keep going and face each challenge head on. Discomfort is temporary but gets easier each day.

– –

Courage

Never be afraid to travel your path alone. Sometimes being alone will bring you the awareness you need to overcome challenges and obstacles. Solitude can bring about clarity, and show you what needs to be done in order to move forwards. We all feel lonely at times, but rest assured you will find friends who will fit in with your new beliefs and your new way of living. Until then, find the healing you need and enjoy time alone to gather your life together, and to prepare for the new journey ahead.

− −

Open your eyes and see a new path before you. Take a chance and keep going, because what's ahead can only be better than what's behind you. What happened, happened for a reason; it's now time to forge ahead into new beginnings. Don't be afraid; your time is now.

− −

When life feels messy

Stop being afraid of your potential and start believing in yourself. You are capable of so much more than you think. Stop doubting and start doing what it is you want to do.

– –

Never be afraid to say what you need to say. Don't let others belittle your thoughts or words. If there's something you need to say, don't hold it in; speak up and be heard, for what you have to say is important.

– –

Fear will hold you back. Courage and determination will move you forward. Be the change you wish to see in your world because only you can fight for the life you want. First, discard the old and walk away from the life you have lived, so that you can begin something wonderfully new. It will all be worth it in the end.

– –

Courage

Fear of failure can take over and hold you down. Finding the courage to actually step out and make your dreams come true, is easier once you realise that fear is only an illusion of your thoughts. Don't let those thoughts stop you; take the plunge and get back on the path that will lead you to your dreams. You can do it.

– –

Don't give your power to others by reacting to their thoughts. Stay strong and walk away. There's no need to defend yourself against the little minds of others.

– –

When life feels messy

It takes great courage to step away from all you know, but it is worth it. It can be hard and lonely starting on a new path, because as you start to find new interests, people you hold dear may fall away. It's like you're being stripped bare and have to start over again, which can be scary; but know that you can do it if you choose to, especially if you use all your power and determination to get to where you want to go. The steps you take now will take you very far indeed. Believe in yourself, you know you want this. Keep pushing forward, and going with the flow. There will be times when you do travel backwards but know that it's okay, because sometimes you need to learn more lessons before you can walk away.

– –

Courage

Be true to yourself and stay strong. There are many out there that will try and take away your power by bringing you down or by doing or saying things that will hurt you. Know that this has nothing to do with you, and everything to do with them; it's their fears and insecurities that are being brought to the surface and being directed at you, because they choose not to see this inside themselves and are not fixing their own lives. You are stronger than this and deserve to hold yourself to a higher place. Stay strong and walk away from negative situations and people who belittle you and take away your worth. It's okay to walk away in order to save yourself.

– –

When life feels messy

Sometimes you have to swallow your pride and just say what's on your mind. Even if others don't like hearing what you say, at least you've expressed what's in your heart. Speak your mind and stand by your truth – even if your voice shakes while you do it.

– –

In the fiery depths of your soul lies a beautiful power within, a power that allows you to create anything your heart desires. A power to heal all that you've wanted to heal. Be brave and courageous, because as soon as you face it, you will gain new clarity, more strength, and a whole new you. Nothing that you have faced in the past has the power to hold you back, it's only your thoughts, and your perceptions and limiting beliefs.

– –

Courage

Let go of people, let go of control, let go of unhealthy situations and decide to be free. Stop holding on, stop pressing the replay button, and step out of the circle you've been living in for so long. You are too important in this world to let yourself be pulled down by others.

– –

Sometimes we need to let go of certain people and situations in order to move on. We have to leave people from the past, our old beliefs and parts of our personality behind, in order to wake up to the world that surrounds us. Once you welcome the ending of an old life and the birthing of a new one, you'll rise from the ashes like a phoenix, enabling you to spread your wings and fly high.

– –

When life feels messy

Dare to be different. Step out of the every day norm of life and shake up your life by doing something totally out of the ordinary. What is something that you've always dreamed of doing, but never have due to excuses? Today is the day to do it, so stop letting the insecurities take over your mind. You can do anything you desire if you set your mind on your goals. Go for it, the time is now. What have you got to lose?

– –

If there is something that you feel you need to do, because it will benefit your soul, then do it. Have the courage to do what you feel is right for you, and don't let guilt or external circumstances stop you. Your soul will thank you for doing so.

– –

Courage

You can't keep running away from your problems because they will eventually show up in your life again. To heal, simply turn around and face them head on. Find the lessons, face the pain, accept that it's happened and start forgiving yourself and others. There's no point in running because it will just wear you down. Be strong and face the thing you fear the most. Let yourself feel all the emotions you need to, lean on someone if you need help, but stop running because life will eventually get on top of you if you don't.

– –

We all have a story to share, don't be afraid to come out and share it with others. By sharing your story, you may be helping others along their path. You are an inspiration no matter how big or small your story is.

– –

When life feels messy

Just because something seems big and scary doesn't mean it is. It is our mind that has placed these fears inside us, so embrace them, thank them, and then let them go. For it is through your fears that you can learn so much. Let your fears teach you that this is not how you want to be.

– –

It's time to start listening to your heart and start reaching for your dreams. You've been waiting for the right moment for so long but nothing has come about. You can only start living the life of your dreams when you decide to make it happen. It's no good sitting around waiting for it to happen, you have to make it happen. Don't be scared of the unknown, it's a wonderful feeling to follow your heart and chase your dreams.

– –

Courage

Be brave enough to listen to your inner voice that says, "Go on, and give it a try; what have you got to lose?" Listen to the voice that encourages you to walk further along your path, and ignore those thoughts that try to belittle you and tell you that you are not good enough. You are good enough to achieve anything you desire, so roar like a lion and move forward on the path in the direction of your dreams. That little voice inside of you will soon become so loud that you will wonder why you never listened to it in the first place.

– –

When life feels messy

Take a chance and leap into the unknown. When you step out of your comfort zone miracles appear. Be brave, take a stand, do something different and trust that you will be fully guided along your desired path. Let go of the fears that hold you back, holding on to those fears is like caging yourself in a prison. Take a leap of faith and you'll feel the freedom within take hold.

– –

Determination

When life feels messy

The more you deny yourself, the more you'll find yourself becoming disheartened. Follow your bliss, wherever that may take you.

– –

When life knocks you down, pick yourself up, dust yourself off and start over. Life is about changing and moving forward. When things don't work out, this is for a reason. You may not understand it now but your life will get better if you keep trying. Never give up – on yourself.

– –

Your goals are not meant to be hard, the obstacles you face are not meant to deter you; instead they are meant to push you further on towards making your dreams a reality. Stay determined and always keep your eye on the end result.

– –

Determination

Sometimes in life there may be things that you won't like but you may have to do. Instead of complaining about the task ahead, why not try and just do it. The more you complain the more the task will seem difficult. Accept what you have to do and try to get through without complaining, you never know it could be a blessing.

– –

In the darkness of it all, one seed of hope can sprout new beginnings. Feed that hope and inside will grow a mountain of love for yourself and all who surround you. Let that seed flourish, nurture it, talk to it, love it, feed it. So many possibilities can spring from one small seed. Give it light, give it love and it will grow.

– –

When life feels messy

Stop beating yourself up. Stop living in the past and start living in the now; your future depends on it. The Universe is waiting for you. You deserve to have everything you want, and you can if you stop hiding away in your thoughts and letting your fears take over.

– –

You are capable of doing the one thing you feared to do. Banish the negative thoughts from your mind, stop letting fear take hold, and step over your fears right now. Believe in yourself, you can do anything you set your mind to.

– –

Realise that every day is a new chance to start over and try again. Stay determined and believe that you will get through whatever it is you are experiencing.

– –

Determination

Never let the fire of passion go out within you. Strive to be all you can be and never give up on following your dreams. You just have to believe in what you're doing.

– –

It's never too late to start following your dream or starting over. If things fall apart don't be disheartened; instead, let it make you more determined. Mistakes can be blessings in disguise; you just have to recognise them.

– –

You have to do what's right for you. If you know it and feel it with everything you have inside, then follow it. Don't look back, just trust yourself; only you will know if it's the right thing to do. You can invite other people's opinions but in the end it ultimately all comes down to you. Trust your gut because it will never steer you wrong.

– –

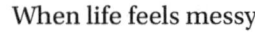

When life feels messy

Never give up on your hopes, dreams and wishes. Never give up on yourself, because if you do, you'll find it hard to pull yourself up. Always believe that your dreams are worth fighting for, and that YOU are worth fighting for.

– –

Standing still won't get you anywhere; you have to keep moving forward in order to achieve your dreams. So whatever you do today, travel with a smile on your face, and confidence in your heart.

– –

It doesn't matter how slow you go, as long as you keep climbing. Perseverance is what will get you to your heaven on earth. Keep moving forward, keep reaching for your goal; it takes hard work but the end result is so worth it.

– –

Determination

Don't be ashamed or embarrassed about crying; it's perfectly normal. Just be proud that you can keep going through the storm.

– –

Sometimes you need to hit rock bottom before you can appreciate your life or see your own greatness. Rock bottom can be the very thing you need to realise the strength and determination you have inside. Never think that you'll be at rock bottom forever; it's merely a destination to help you realise who you really are, and to show you what you're worth.

– –

The Universe is always working to make your dreams come true. Make a promise to yourself to keep working on you, and you will find that as things progress, so too will your dreams.

– –

When life feels messy

Fight for your dreams, never give up on achieving what you want and you WILL reach your goals. Don't let anything or anyone get in the way of your dreams, you deserve to achieve your dreams, you only have one life, so live it the best you can.

– –

Forgive yourself for falling down and be proud of yourself for getting back up and trying again.

– –

You can choose to stay stuck in the weeds of your past and let them grow all over you, or you can choose to cut them down and move forward fearlessly. Once you take that first step out of the wilderness, you will never look back. Have faith and be brave; you have more strength and willpower than you realise.

– –

Determination

Do the best you can and be the best you can be. Make the most of your life on your terms and in your own time. Don't follow others, make your own path and never give up.

– –

If you don't go for what you want, someone else will. Take the necessary steps to achieve them and listen to that little voice inside that says, "Go For It!"

– –

Persistence and determination will always see you reach your destination. Don't let the stones that life throws at you get in your way. If need be, jump over them or even better, smash through them!

– –

When life feels messy

Don't let the hard work put you off, instead think about your end goal and go for it. When you think about the work you have to do to reach your goal, you'll probably be put off and maybe even give up. Thinking about the end result and visualising yourself already there helps push you further towards your goal. Keep striving and you'll get there.

– –

Do not let others lead you off your path. Stay strong, stand your ground; only you know where you're going. They can either be happy for you, or they can stay stuck in their jealous bubble, but that's for them to decide. There is no need for you to take on their feelings. Love yourself and stay true to you.

– –

Determination

Push past the barriers of insecurities and fearful thoughts and start creating your desires.

– –

Don't let one little setback stop you from following your dreams and passions. Get back in there and reharness the determination to make your dreams come true.

– –

Faith

Faith

Walk in blind faith and trust in the path you're on, even if you can't see the road or the destination ahead. Believe that your trust will be rewarded with good things, and that everything will work out perfectly.

– –

Awaken yourself, for you are a magical being who can create endless opportunities; you just have to believe in yourself. Believe you can achieve anything, believe you can break through any obstacle, and you will.

– –

Faith will always carry you through. The only way to quieten your fears is to overcome them.

– –

You place fears in your thoughts, so if you can work to lose those thoughts then you'll also lose those fears.

– –

When life feels messy

Know that you are divinely loved, supported and protected as you travel along your path. Everything you are going through right now is for a purpose. Even if you can't see the reasons for it all, trust that they will be revealed to you when you are ready.

– –

We are all intuitive, the challenge is to silence the mind enough to hear it and then trust what you are hearing.

– –

Release the need to control everything. Let go of your expectations and how you want things to be, and just go with the flow. Things may not turn out how we want them to, but they will turn out the way they are meant to be.

– –

Faith

Just because things gets dark and you can't see what's happening in life, don't give up and throw it all away. Stay on the path and trust the Universe will lead you where you need to be.

– –

Nothing is ever a coincidence and nothing ever happens by chance. Everything you go through happens for a reason, because there are lessons to learn and people to learn from.

– –

Your angels are trying to send you messages. To hear them, quieten your mind, breathe, and listen to your heart. Your angels are always with you, so if ever you need help, all you need to do is ask and be open to their response.

– –

When life feels messy

Even if you can't see it within yourself, know that you are a miracle created by the Universe. You have been put on this earth to shine and shine you will. You don't need miracles to happen; you just need to see yourself as the miracle you are. Once you do that, your life will take you to amazing places.

– –

When you quieten your mind and listen, what do you hear? Take a deep breath and then slowly release it. Listen to the beat of your heart and it will whisper to you, it's purest desires. Your heart will always tell you where to go next. Don't be afraid to hear its truth; you can trust the love in your heart because it will never let you down.

– –

Faith

Trust in the process of your life. There may be things we will never understand fully, but trust that what you are going through is for your highest good; even if it feels terrible and you can't see a way out. Remember, after every storm the sun always shines.

– –

Everything is going to be fine, you'll see. Trust that all will work out for you, and that you will receive what you need. Believe, let go, and have faith. You will get there; just don't give up.

– –

Another new week, and another new day where anything you put your mind to is achievable. Make the most of how you live your day, follow your dreams all the way, and have full faith that when you follow your heart's desires, your dreams will come true.

– –

Patience is critical. You don't always need to know your next step in life. Sometimes you just have to wait and see what unfolds. Trust that things will work out and your God, angels, spirit, source, and the Universe, will lead you. You will know when it's the right time to move forward, you will get sudden thoughts, feelings, maybe even visions – a sudden knowing. Trust, have faith, but for now get back to enjoying life, get outside, play with your kids or loved ones; find something to do to take your mind off "the next step", and your answers will probably come to you when you least expect it.

– –

Faith

Have patience that your manifestations are being worked out for you by the Universe. When you fully let go, you are trusting in the Divine to work for you. Your prayers will always be answered. Leave it all up to your angels. Can you see the butterflies? They are your angels delivering your dreams to you. Let go, trust and believe.

– –

Have faith in all you do and what you're working towards, and trust that things will get better. Believe in the unbelievable for when you hold those feelings and beliefs your desires will come about faster. Stop focusing on the negatives and keep your mind and thoughts positive. When you focus on "what if something goes wrong?" you will bring negativity into your life. Where are your thoughts?

– –

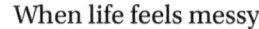
When life feels messy

Trust your heart, and you will never be steered in the wrong direction. Your heart will always tell you right from wrong, but sometimes you just need to be silent in order to hear its gentle whispers of encouragement.

— —

Sometimes you have to take a step back and think to yourself, "am I being helped or being pulled down?" The people who pull you down are the ones that you need to let go of. Your heart knows what's right and what's wrong; you just have to listen to it.

— —

Do you feel the nudges towards people or places, which the Universe is providing? Don't question it, just do it. You may not see the reasons at the time, but trust that it will all make sense in the end. Go with the flow and let the Universe guide you to where you need to go.

— —

Faith

Even in the most trying times you are never alone, there is always someone to help you along the way. You may not see them but they are there with you every step of the way.

– –

There is no right or wrong path, so wherever you choose to go, know that it will always lead you to where you are supposed to be.

– –

Trust what the Universe is telling you; trust your angels, trust your body, and trust your heart. When you see the signs or hear the messages, don't think too much about it (or you'll risk over-analysing it); instead, have faith that if it feels right, then it is right.

– –

When life feels messy

The answers to your whole existence will not show themselves to you all at once. Instead, they will appear throughout your journey when challenges arise. You will find all the answers that you seek, just have patience, trust and faith in your path. Everything will unfold as you move through life.

– –

Never be afraid to look within. You may find things you don't like about yourself but these are opportunities to improve or heal yourself. Whenever you seek answers, look deep inside and you'll find them.

– –

Faith

The Universe has something amazing planned for you. The thing is, you're not supposed to know the plan, you're just supposed to live it. Trust that all will be wonderful; simply follow your heart and you will soon see for yourself.

– –

Believe in yourself, believe in your dreams; take it step-by-step and you will eventually get there.

– –

Practise patience and believe that everything will work out in its own time. Sometimes when we rush things, we miss the inner guidance from above, so slow down and take the time to hear the gentle whispers from God.

– –

Follow the guidance of your heart rather than the small negative thoughts in your mind.

– –

You are the Divine. You are love and you are light. See this within yourself like others see it within you. Be at peace with yourself. Listen to your heart. Go forward fearlessly, knowing that you are supported every step of the way.

– –

Believe that something wonderful is going to happen. There are miracles around us everyday and it will happen to you; just be patient. Have hope, have faith; your miracle is coming.

– –

Faith

Sometimes all you need to do is take a minute to pray. When you ask God, your angels or whoever it is you believe in, your prayers will be answered. If you stop and listen to your heart, you will realise that the answers always lie within.

– –

Don't get lost in hopelessness just because you can't see immediate results. Results take time to manifest. Have patience for now, and enjoy each moment, because when you are still, you'll hear the whispers of your heart guiding you to your next step.

– –

Have faith that things are always falling into place. The Universe has a plan for you; you just need to release some control and trust that what is meant to happen, will.

– –

When life feels messy

Trust that someone will come along at exactly the right moment. You don't need to go searching; just enjoy your life and love will find you when the time is right. There is always someone out there, waiting to connect with you.

– –

Believe in the path you're on and trust that you are going in the right direction. There is no right or wrong choice; every situation you are faced with is there to learn from. Whatever you are faced with can be resolved with love and compassion. You can either fight it or just go with it.

– –

Notice your thoughts when your mind wanders because this is where your heart's true desires lay; your dreams, imagination and intuition will always lead you there.

– –

Faith

Believe with your entire heart that you can do and be anything you want. When you believe with all your soul, you'll start to bring your dream to life, because what you think about you will create.

– –

Things in life may not turn out the way you want them to, but always remember that things will turn out the way they are meant to. So let go of control and see where life takes you. Accept where it leads you; don't focus on why it didn't work out the way you wanted it to and instead, focus on where you are at this point in time and fully embrace it, knowing it's where you're meant to be right now.

– –

Trust yourself enough to know that you are headed in the right direction. Your heart will lead you to where you belong.

– –

When life feels messy

Sometimes you just have to go with your gut and trust that it will lead you to the right places or people. When you think too much about decisions you can over-analyse and make the wrong choice. So next time you are in the thick of it and your gut tells you to do something, go ahead and do it, knowing that your decision is the right one.

– –

In the silence of breath is where we hear our true guidance from our creator. Stop for a moment, let your mind be still, and listen to the beating sound of your heart and listen for the messages she gently beats to you. It's here you will find answers to your most pressing problems.

– –

Faith

Life is not meant to be figured out; instead we're meant to learn how to "go with the flow". Unlike a movie where there's a script to follow, in life we just have to listen to our hearts and have faith we are being led in the right direction.

– –

Keep on moving, keep on trying, and never give up on what you want or what you believe in. Have faith that you will get there in the end. If you give up before the rainbow shines, you can only ever stay stuck in the storm.

– –

Don't take notice of criticism; it's someone else's problem, not yours. Know that there will always be people who want to try and bring you down. Don't buy into what others think of you – their opinion of you is actually none of your business!

– –

As soon as you ask for it, if it's meant to be, the Universe, your angels or your God will conspire to make it happen. It may be drawn out and you may have to go through more waiting, or even more darkness, but keep faith that it will happen the way it's meant to.

– –

Never stop believing that you will get there, God and your angels are working behind the scenes to ensure that everything is working out for you. Sometimes it takes a lot of patience to arrive where you are meant to be, but know that with patience and never-ending determination, you will get there.

– –

Anything is possible if you just dream and believe. Visualise your dreams coming true and hold on to those dreams and visualisations. Keep talking to your angels and have faith that they are working behind the scenes to help you on your path.

– –

Faith

Everything is going to be all right, have a little faith and trust in what you can't see. Let go and let God work everything out for you.

– –

When you surrender your problems to the Universe, you will start to see the signs and guidance leading you along to the next step on your path.

– –

Trust what your intuition is telling you, have faith that your heart will lead you where you need to be.

– –

Even if you don't know if you have done the right thing, sometimes you just have to pray and have faith that you have done the right thing. It will all make sense in the end as nothing that is decided in life is ever a mistake, it's all there to guide you on your path.

– –

When life feels messy

Taking the time to walk away from a situation for a while can bring things back into perspective. It is the process of letting go and detaching yourself that will give you a new sense of direction. When it all seems confusing and tiring, give yourself permission to walk away, and you will find that what you think is a problem, isn't really a problem at all, but a blessing in disguise.

– –

Every step you take towards making your dreams and desires come true, is a huge accomplishment in itself. Even if it feels like it's taking you forever, know that you are travelling at the pace you're supposed to and trust that you will get there when the time is right.

– –

Faith

When things seem like they are falling apart, accept it and know that a new and brighter beginning will enter your life. You will soon see the hidden blessings behind it all, and you will come out stronger and on top. Have patience and never let your faith or hope diminish. Keep that beacon of light burning inside of you.

– –

Sometimes in life all you can do is close your eyes, clear your heart, and let it all go. We often try so hard to control everything at all times, when sometimes all we actually need to do is let it go. Things will work out the way they're supposed to.

– –

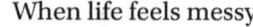

When all else fails, stop for a moment and look within. Put your inner thoughts aside and instead listen to your heart. What is your gut feeling telling you? Your heart will always know, so just breathe and let it guide your way. Trust and have faith in your soul, for your soul is your heart trying to get your attention. Follow it, as it will never steer you wrong.

– –

Know that you have the strength within to overcome all obstacles you are faced with, because if God didn't believe in you, He wouldn't have placed them before you. All of your obstacles are meant to be overcome, don't give in and don't give up, keep fighting through and always believe that things will get better.

– –

Faith

Hold faith that whatever you are working towards is coming about, keep your thoughts positive, and always believe that everything you go through is a blessing. Keep moving forward on your desired path and trust that everything is unfolding exactly as it should be.

– –

Leaving the comforts of your old life can be scary, but surrendering the old and walking away to start a new path is a wonderful feeling. Doors will open, and things will happen that you would never have thought possible. Have faith and trust that your new path will take you to beautiful places.

– –

When life feels messy

The sun will always shine for you, even if you can't see it. Have faith that life gets better, believe that through your darkest days there will always be a rainbow there to lighten up your day. This too shall pass, as with every tide turning, every blade of grass growing, life is always changing, know that you can't stay stuck there forever, unless you choose to do so. You have the power to pull yourself out of the dark recesses of your mind; you have the strength and resolve to let the light shine through to you. Never give up hope, and never stop believing, there's always a pinch of fairy dust within you waiting to sparkle up your day. Things will get better.

– –

Doors of opportunity are always open, be brave enough to walk through them, and trust that when you do, you will be led to even more magical moments.

– –

Faith

Stop doubting yourself and start believing in you. Have confidence in what you say and what you do. The moment you start doubting yourself heaviness sets in and starts to bring you down and you may find it hard to pull yourself out. Everything you set out to do is for the greatest good of all, and in time you will see that this path you've been led to, was all for a reason that benefits not only you, but everyone else that you come across.

– –

If your world seems small and dark right now, have faith in the Universe and trust that you are being led to something more wonderful. Because "this too shall pass." There is always light after the storm when rainbows appear, and it will be magnificent once you reach it. Just hold on and believe you will – because you will.

– –

When life feels messy

There are no other paths than the one you are on right now. The path you travel is the one you're meant to experience.

– –

The door to life is always open, you just have to be brave enough to walk through it and allow yourself to receive all the goodness life is waiting to give you. It's all there at your fingertips; right within your reach. Surrender the hurt, the pain and allow yourself this wonderful gift. Life is truly beautiful when you're ready for it, but first you have to let go of all that weighs you down.

– –

It does get better; things always have a way of working out. Put your faith in God and trust that He will help you through. In the meantime, stay strong, positive and believe that anything is possible.

– –

Faith

The positive thing about storms is that they always pass; they never last forever and just at the end of it, blue skies, rainbows and sunshine always appear. Hold on tight through your storms because wonderful things will follow.

– –

Just as your physical wounds take time to heal, so too does your heart. Give yourself time to heal, and don't push yourself. Things will get better and you will see the rainbow after the storm; nothing stays the same forever.

– –

Yes you were and ARE strong enough to get through anything. You've come this far so don't give up on yourself now. Keep holding onto hope and faith inside of you, never letting it go. Hold faith that you will come out stronger and better, knowing that there are wonderful things in store for you.

– –

You will never know unless you give it a try. Why hold on to those thoughts about whether or not you think something may be right or maybe wrong for you? Until you have a go you will never know. Take a leap of faith; you never know where you might land.

— —

Always believe that something magical is about to happen, for it is always happening at every moment, every hour, every minute. It happens for everyone and it will happen for you. Believe, hold on and have faith.

— —

Have faith that your dreams are coming true. Keep going with the positive affirmations and visualisations, because the more you work with manifesting those dreams, the faster they come about. Trust that it will work out as it's meant to.

— —

Faith

You are the mapmaker of your destiny. You have everything you need to make your dreams come true. Stay on your path and know that all the twists and turns will define who you are. Everywhere you go and everyone you meet is there for you to learn from. Stand tall and strong in your beliefs, stay positive, go with the flow, and don't bend to anyone's will. Let the destination drive you forward, but also let the journey mould you into the person you will become.

– –

This is a sign for you to stop fighting and holding on to all those struggles in life. It's a reminder to get down and pray to your God and your angels and ask them to take over and guide you to what's right for you; trust that they will lead you to where you are meant to be.

– –

When life feels messy

Follow your intuition and trust what your heart is telling you. When you follow your heart you are allowing your intuition to get stronger. The more you trust yourself the more life will go the way you want. When making decisions, take a moment to breathe and listen to your heart's stirrings. If it feels right within all your being, go for it. If it feels wrong stay well clear of it. Your heart always knows the answer.

— —

Today is a new day and a perfect day to start trusting yourself and what your heart wants. Start trusting your gut instincts. Don't deny yourself or your heart; you are here to learn and evolve. You need to trust in order to move forward.

— —

Faith

Be thankful for this day that God has given you and be grateful for all the blessings He has bestowed upon you. There are always blessings to be thankful for, no matter what is going on in your life. Even the trials you go through have blessings in them. Sometimes you just can't see the reason behind them yet, but don't worry, within time you will realise what they are.

– –

It's sad when we see people we love follow paths that don't serve them well, especially when you want to help but can't. In such an instance, all you can do is pray that they will find the peace that they are looking for in life, and have faith that they're on a journey they're supposed to be on. Send them love, hope for the best, and never give up the belief that they will find their inner light, because all things are possible.

– –

When life feels messy

Have faith and trust that everything is working out for your highest good. Take time out and focus on believing. When you focus on the negatives then your dreams will take longer to manifest. Have faith that what you want is just around the corner and soon you will start to see your steps falling into place; trust that you will be led in the right direction.

– –

Listen to your inner voice, to your heart, your angels, your intuition. Stop, breathe and hear the answers within; have faith and trust that your heart is telling you the right thing.

– –

If things don't work out the way you want, know that it is because something better is being planned for you by a higher power that you can't yet see. If it didn't happen,v it's not meant to right now; leave it to God to give you what you need.

– –

Forgiveness

When life feels messy

Until to you learn to let go of the past and all that weighs you down, you can never learn to fly, and you'll never see what the Universe can give you.

– –

Forgive yourself so that you can start to heal. Forget the past mistakes of what you should or shouldn't have done, because it's not worth holding onto that pain any longer. Until you forgive yourself, you'll only stay in your mental anguish. It's time to heal, release your pain, and free yourself from your past so that new and wonderful beginnings can emerge.

– –

When you forgive, you start to let go and release all the anger towards others and yourself. Your heart starts to heal, and happiness creeps back inside and takes over.

– –

Forgiveness

Everyone needs forgiveness no matter what they've done in the past. Everyone is fighting their own battles, and everything happens for a reason. Forgive others so that you can move on, and forgive yourself in order to heal. When you hold onto anger and resentment you feed the situation, which in turn makes you remain connected with it. Freedom begins with you, and it all starts with forgiveness.

– –

Forgive them even if they're not sorry, because doing so will help you move forwards in your own life. When you do not forgive, resentment can confine you in a state of negativity. Forgive so that you can be free.

– –

When life feels messy

Release the past, release the pain and anger that you hold on to. Keep the memories and move on. When you hold on to the negatives emotions of the past, you'll leave no room for the new to enter. Give yourself the freedom you need and deserve, so that you can move forward and welcome new experiences into your world.

– –

Sometimes when we look back on things in our life we feel sadness for the things that have happened. It's okay to feel this way, as long as you forgive yourself for it; if you don't, the guilt could eat you up inside. If you need to forgive yourself repeatedly until you know you've moved on from it, then do so. Just tell yourself "I love you for everything you've been through, and I hold no judgement against you". What's done is done, so feel the sadness if you need to, but then move on from it.

– –

Forgive yourself. There is no need to keep holding onto the suppressed guilt you hold so tightly inside your heart. You are doing the best you can. Can you see that the pain that you're going through is actually good for you, because it helps you to see where you need to make changes? It feels like you are on a constant climb, but keep climbing, because you will get there, and you will see the sun shine through the darkness that surrounds you.

– –

Freedom can come at any time YOU choose to leave the past behind. It can be hard to see the other through the eyes of God if anger is in the way, but once you let that anger go, you are on your way to being free. Let go, even if it's just a little bit at a time, so that you can start to heal and move on.

– –

Gratitude

Gratitude

Consider yourself very blessed, if those you treat harshly choose to stick around, for they have seen beyond your imperfections and love you for who you truly are, and not how you've treated or are treating them.

– –

It is important to take time out to see the beauty in the world that surrounds you. Watch a sunrise or sunset, observe the vibrant colours of nature's changing seasons, or count the stars on a moonless night. Enjoy the gift of life that you've been given, and all it has to offer. Get out in nature and feel the beauty that is all around you.

– –

When life feels messy

Understand that all the pain, laughter, tears and love is worth it. Feel grateful that you shared a part of your life with someone because what you had provided lessons, made you stronger, helped you grow, and taught you love and compassion. Towards the end, the Universe saw that you had forged different paths to start your new journeys in life. So take a moment to thank them for being part of your life, because they have helped you become the person you are today.

– –

When that magical moment occurs, and the light shines down on you and wakes you up for a new day, say to yourself: "I am alive and grateful for every experience, because without them, I wouldn't be who I am today".

– –

Gratitude

Be grateful for where you are right now, and focus on today instead of tomorrow. You only have this moment now, just be, and be grateful for all of the lessons you have learned, conquered and survived. You are stronger and more capable than you realise.

– –

Today is a day to begin again, to let go of old behaviours, thoughts and patterns. Embrace each new day as a gift, because every day you wake up breathing IS something to be thankful for.

– –

See everything in your life as a blessing. Whatever you've experienced was all meant to be, and will continue to be. Treat the past with gratitude because it's made you into the beautiful soul you are today.

– –

When life feels messy

What matters most right now is what you have. Be grateful for the blessings already bestowed upon you, because there are millions out there that don't even have a quarter of what you have. What you have is what matters; you are rich compared to others. Be happy and grateful.

— —

Never forget to look back on your past every now and then and thank it for bringing you to where you are today. Without your past you wouldn't have learned all the wisdom you have today. Even though the past can be traumatic, it is your blessing. You may not have liked the lessons but you have learned so much from it all. Do not look at how far you still have to go, instead look at how far you have come on this journey through life, be proud of yourself and celebrate what you've achieved.

— —

Count your blessings and be grateful for everything that you already have in your life. When you show and feel gratitude for what you have, you attract more good into your life. It's easy to forget to be grateful when you focus on things that you don't have; but by focusing on what you do have, you'll bring yourself back to the present.

– –

Gratitude is something we forget from time to time when we are trying to visualise our future. Write down all you are grateful for, because one day it might be taken away from you. Practise gratitude for the things you have every single day, and your life will become brighter.

– –

There is always something to be grateful for. Sometimes it may be hard to focus on positive thoughts when all that's happening around is negative, but find the positive in every situation. If you don't open your eyes and see the lesson you will never learn.

– –

Don't forget to breathe. Take your mind off of your worries and focus on the present moment. Look at your surroundings and remind yourself what you have to feel grateful for.

– –

Are you truly appreciative for what you already have? Instead of wishing for more things, be grateful for what you already have. This will help you see the beauty in your life.

– –

Gratitude

Express your gratitude. Feel it rise up within you from the very depths of your soul and sing it out loud. When you view your life with gratitude, it puts you on a never-ending wave of happiness.

– –

Look at how far you've come on the road you've travelled. Be proud of all you've achieved. Let yourself feel joy and pride in seeing what you've accomplished. Your efforts deserve to be recognised so don't dismiss them as nothing. Pat yourself on the back, lift your vibrations, and be thankful for what you've been through because it got you to where you are now.

– –

Don't lose hope. Show gratitude and be grateful for all that's happened and while you wait for the Universe's plan to unfold, go out and enjoy your life.

– –

When life feels messy

Be grateful for everything you have in your life. If you can't find gratitude then imagine your world without all the things you have.

– –

Look around you, what do you see? There are so many things to be grateful for, the bed you sleep in, clothes on your back, food you eat, the car you drive, family and friends who have huge amounts of love for you, the great blue sky and that gorgeous shining orb that twinkles high, the smell of flowers, and so much more. Take time out from the stresses in your mind and bring yourself back to this present moment by looking around you and be grateful for all that you have. Remember, there are so many others out there right now that don't even have half as much as you.

– –

Gratitude

Sometimes people will come into your life for a short period only to leave again. Don't be sad for their departure, instead feel grateful that they were there in the first place. Every person who comes into your life is there to help you move forwards on your path – be it good or bad. Accept that this is so and send them love, no matter what they have helped you with, because you will have evolved in some way.

– –

Find the beauty in everything that surrounds you. Appreciate that even the ugliest things are born from love and beauty.

– –

Everyday is a day worth celebrating. Each day you wake up alive and breathing is a day to be thankful for. Sing, dance, scream and shout; shout your gratitude from the heart and feel that your soul has been smiling all along.

– –

Acquiring more material possessions won't make you happy, it just fills a temporary void until you want more. When you feel grateful for what you have, you'll realise that you have everything you need.

– –

Even if you are going through a hard time right now, stop for a minute and take a look around you. Notice the sun, the moon, the clouds and all of nature. Look beyond and you will see that there is so much to be grateful for in your life. There is always something to give thanks for.

– –

Be grateful that every past experience you have ever been through has brought you to where you are today. Because without those past experiences you would never learn or grow, and you wouldn't be the person you are today.

– –

Gratitude

Even if you are going through a hard time right now, stop for a minute and take a look around you. Notice the sun, the moon, the clouds and all of nature. Look far and wide, and you will see that there is so much to be grateful for in your life. There is always something to give thanks for.

– –

Be grateful for all you have, because one day you might wake and find that it's all gone. Stop wishing for more, and take a good hard look at your surroundings. Imagine if it were all taken away. What would life be like then? Today is a great day to appreciate everything you have in your life.

– –

When life feels messy

Stop complaining about life, and be content with where you are. Look around you and be grateful. Be grateful for what you have. While at times it may be hard, and the things we go through can really pull us down, be grateful for the life you are living. Look around you, look around your house, your relationships, and be grateful for all that you have because there are so many people in this world that don't have half as much as what you have. You have so much!
– –

Gratitude

Put one hand on your heart and one on your belly. Can you feel the beat of your heart? Can you feel the rise and fall of your breath? Guess what, you are alive, and there is nothing else more satisfying than that! Express your gratitude with all that's around you and give thanks to the Universe for fully supplying you with all your needs and wants.

– –

Give thanks for all you have and give thanks for all you've been through. The hard times are what helps you grow and makes you stronger.

– –

Life

Life

You will never find true happiness in your life by seeking it with another unless you have truly loved and accepted yourself for who you are. No one else can make you happy; no one else can fix your world but YOU.

– –

You can't fill the hole in your life with material things. Be strong and keep moving on your path, find yourself and heal, and eventually all will fall into place. For now, focus on fixing YOU. Don't look to others or seek out things to fill the void. The answer lies within.

– –

Somewhere out there in the world someone is fighting to live, and wanting and needing what you already have. Bring yourself back to the present moment and remember gratitude for the things you already have in your world.

– –

You are never too old to change your ways. As long as you keep working towards your intentions and desired outcomes you will get there. But first, you have to start the change within yourself to get to where you want to go. It can be hard letting go of old thought patterns and behaviours but it can be done. Keep moving forwards, stay strong, age is not a barrier; you can achieve the impossible when you put your heart and soul into it.

– –

Today is a new and unique day that you can fill with many wonderful things. Make it amazing by trying new things and by taking the steps to achieve your dreams. Feel grateful for every day.

– –

Life

If you want to learn how to ride a bike, buy one. If you want to learn how to ride a horse, take lessons. If you want to learn how to cook, buy a cookbook. If you want to be kind to others, start with one word of kindness. If you want to know how to love, open your heart. If you want to change your life then take one step at a time. As with all things in life, learning new skills will take time; but with practise each day, life will get better.

– –

You can't control other people's thoughts, words, or the way they act, but you can control how you react. Don't let yourself be pulled into anyone else's dramas; put yourself first and walk away from anything that's not worth your precious time.

– –

You have so much beauty inside but yet you deny yourself true happiness and peace. Leave the past where it belongs and come join the healing embrace of the angels. They'll gently guide you along when you surrender to the past.

– –

Life is too short to sit by the wayside and just watch the world go by. You have to get out there and live like you've never lived before – as if it were your last day.

– –

It's not all about reaching your destination; it's about how well you travel between each state. When you become at one with your journey, the more you will awaken the true beauty of life.

– –

Life

Let yourself feel all the emotions you need to. There's no point in holding anything in; if you need to cry, shout, yell or scream, do it; give it to the Universe so that you can release it, and the Universe will turn it into something you need. The more you deny yourself and hold it all in, the longer and harder it will be for you to let go, and the more damage it may do.

– –

Think back to the time you were born and remember the wonderful being that you were – so full of love, light and innocence. Stop drowning yourself and just live; there's no time like the present to return to innocence and beauty. You are everything and more – you just have to remember that, and believe it.

– –

Act like everything is a miracle and in turn you will see yourself as the miracle. Don't give up on yourself, believe with all your heart that you are a blessing in this world, for you truly are, even if you can't feel it.

– –

Today is a perfect day to bring your focus back to the present moment and remind yourself about all the wonderful things that you already have in your life. Be mindful of your thoughts and observe where you're focusing your attention. Are you focusing on negative or positive thoughts? What you think about, you will create more of in your life.

– –

Life

Your world will respond so much better to you when you stop pretending to be someone you're not. You are absolutely awesome just the way you are. Life is magical when you are being true to yourself, so show the real you, don't be shy, step out of the shadows and just be YOU.

– –

Love, gratitude, compassion, forgiveness, kindness, respect, joy, happiness, even sadness, anger and tears are the important experiences. For without these, it is impossible to move forwards in life.

– –

Don't look back to yesterday, it is already over, instead be in the now and be present in this very moment in time. You cannot go back and rewrite history for it has already been written. Make today the start of your new life and start living the life you have always dreamed of.

– –

When life feels messy

It's not what you have, or what you look like that makes you a better person. It's also not your skills or where you've been in life; similarly, clothes don't make a person, nor do material goods. It's who you are on the inside; it's your inner soul, and the light within. You are always shining even if you don't feel like you're shining. You are a ray of light, and you are always needed in this world; you are not useless or worthless. You are what makes this world a better place. Keep shining that gorgeous light of yours, keep radiating, and never let yourself dim. There is a place in this beautiful world where you belong.

– –

Life

Life isn't about winning or losing, it's about being the best you can be, and doing the best you can. And if things don't work out the way you had planned or hoped, just remember that you tried your best. For the times you think you have failed, don't be so hard on yourself because sometimes things aren't meant to turn out the way you want them to because there are better things in store for you. Don't be disheartened by what you face now; instead hold onto your hopes and dreams that all is working in divine plan for you. There's always a reason why things do and don't work out.

– –

Sometimes you have to make sacrifices to get to where you want to go. Sometimes you have to give up things to make ends meet, but you know what, maybe it's for your highest good, may be it's a learning curve for you. It doesn't mean it has to stay that way for the long term, it just means that to get what you want out of life, you have to be willing to give up things that are not for your highest good. Perhaps it's just the Universe's way of showing you that there's something better coming into your life when you make room by giving up the old. Don't be frightened to give a little, because you may just receive a whole lot more when you make room and leave the old behind.

– –

Life

All that you have ever been through has been worth it, take a look back and see the blessings of every situation, it was all a gift to you from Heaven above so that you could learn and evolve. You are who you are today because of all you have achieved. You've beaten down the negative barriers and come out on top. Be proud of YOU!

– –

When one door is closing, another one always opens. Do not be afraid of the unseen path before you, many great and magical moments are waiting for you just beyond your reach. Let go of the past with grace and ease and allow new beginnings to take place.

– –

When life feels messy

You are here for a purpose, find your purpose by going inside yourself to seek your answers. It's all there inside you; you have the answers, you just have to still your mind in order to hear them.

– –

Everything will happen when it's meant to. Sometimes certain factors have to fall into place before your desired wish can be fulfilled. Trust that it will, and follow your heart. Everything has its time and place and things can't be rushed. One step at a time, it may take a while or it may come quickly, just be patient and remember that if it's meant to happen, it will.

– –

Life

We are a mirror of others in our lives. There is always something being reflected back to us through others, even when it feels annoying, sad, happy or even angry. You will find that you attract people into your life for a reason. Some may only be short in passing, and some will stay for the long haul, but everyone has qualities that we want or have, and they're all there to help you during your journey, just as you will help them in theirs.

– –

Stop holding on to all that weighs you down and ask your angels for help. Your angels are always there, always willing to lift another angel from their knees. Let go of your struggles and allow yourself to fly.

– –

When life feels messy

Don't let the small-mindedness of one person get you down because there are hundreds of others out there that will lift you up and help you on your way. Stay with the ones who will help you rise, and let go of those who try to bring you down. There's no reason for you to be pulled down to their level; stand up and be strong; walk away while you can, because you deserve to rise up and shine.

– –

Sometimes the things you go through can weigh heavily, but it's how you deal with things that will help you reclaim your power. We all go through things for a reason and you'll find your reasons as time goes on, but for now you have to remember that you can get through anything by believing that there is light at the end; and in the end, light always rules over darkness.

– –

Life

Do something every day that your soul will thank you for. Too often we forget to take time out to do something for ourselves.
Even if it's five minutes a day, you'll benefit greatly from this, as you're giving back to yourself. Don't deny yourself this gift, you are important and you're worth it.

– –

For your own sake – not for the sake of others – live your life with independence and forge your own path. You'll find more appreciation in what surrounds you when you don't let other people's thoughts influence your own feelings.

– –

Love what you do in life and it will always bring you great pleasure. If you're only doing it because you feel you have to, then you'll probably never feel satisfied or happy.

– –

Don't compromise yourself for the sake of others. If something doesn't sit right with you, then try your hardest to stand tall and strong in your truth. You have to do what feels right for you and not for them. Even if you have to kick and shout, always stay strong.

– –

Don't give your power away to those who drive you crazy. Be strong enough to say what you need to say, or stand up and walk away. You can either let them walk all over you or you can do what's right by you, and walk away.

– –

The people who are in your life should be the ones you invest your love and energy in. Forget about the ones from the past, they've taught you lessons and have helped you grow, but now it's time to leave them behind and move on with the ones who remain by your side.

– –

You can never find peace within unless you make peace with your past, accept your past and move on from it. What's done is done and can't be erased, but by accepting it we can find peace.

– –

Life will take you on many twists and turns; the challenge is to flow with it whilst learning through the trials and tribulations you are faced with. Let them empower and enrich you for your life's journey. The more open-hearted and compassionate you are about people and situations that come your way, the more you are able to see that everything and everyone has been a blessing and that they are here to teach you something as you are here to teach them.

– –

When you lie to others you are lying to yourself, and you are also denying yourself the right to express your true self. Don't be ashamed or embarrassed about showing the real you. It's okay to cry, it's okay to show your weaknesses. There is absolutely nothing wrong with it, let your true self be seen and heard, and you will find that people will love and support you more for being you.

– –

You are the writer of your own book. You have the power to make your life the way you want it to be. You may be going through hard times, but have faith that it will all come to an end when you allow it. It's up to you to write your own happy ending.

– –

Life

Why do you hide so much from the world? The world needs your wisdom and love, you are meant to shine; the world needs more angels like you. Be the truest version of yourself and you will find that people will gravitate towards you and you will never be alone again. When you hide you hide your light. Stay true to you and don't conform to other's ideas of how they think you should be. When you do this you are giving away your power. Be yourself, there is no greatest pleasure, love and joy when you are being YOU.

– –

Let yourself feel peace today no matter where you are in life. When you are at peace with yourself, you'll see life with a brand new set of eyes, you'll feel love in your heart, and you'll radiate that out towards others who may be in need. When you feel peace, you are peace.

– –

If there's something that you have been putting off but have wanted to do for ages, then make the time to do it. You are the most important person in your life right now and if you don't look after yourself then you will feel out of balance. Just think of how you will feel after you have done what you wanted. A smile on your face, a skip in your walk, what more could you want? You deserve to have what you want.

– –

Do not judge others by their actions or words; instead send them love with an open heart, for everyone you meet is walking their own path, fighting their own battles. You don't know their travels and will never understand them unless you've walked a mile in their shoes. Be kind, show love, and show compassion to all that you meet.

– –

Life

If people don't find you interesting when you're being your true self, then are they really your friend? When you stop hoping or trying to make people like you, and instead focus on being your authentic self, you'll discover a level of happiness that you haven't experienced before.

– –

Sometimes you just have to give up and walk away; accept the situation for what it is, knowing that you've tried your hardest in that situation. If it won't change then save yourself time and frustration and walk away.

– –

Patience is one of the greatest gifts you can give to others and to yourself. Do not hurry through life; it goes by fast enough as it is.

– –

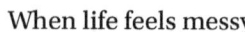

It's never too late to take steps towards making your dreams come true. Regardless of age and experience, if you never follow your heart, you'll never achieve your dreams. Only you can make your dreams come true; but you have to take action.

– –

Every morning when you wake up, decide right then and there that today will be filled with happiness and positivity. When you set your intentions for the day, the Universe conspires to deliver what you've asked for.

– –

No matter how many times you go back to revisit the past, the answer may stay the same. Sometimes you just have to recognise when to let go and move on.

– –

Life

The law of attraction says that when you focus on the negative things that happen in your life, you will attract more negativity. And conversely, by focusing on the positives, you will attract more positive into your life. So what would you rather focus on?

– –

Cast away negative feelings and remember what you deserve in life. You deserve to be happy, so own that happiness now, and live it. Tell yourself "today I choose to be happy. I am happy."

– –

Life is meant to challenge you, we either let the challenges beat us or we can overcome them. If life were meant to be easy we'd all be floating around on fluffy clouds with rainbows in our hair. Embrace the challenges, learn the lessons and take each day as it comes.

– –

Instead of focusing on what lies ahead, try and focus on what lies within. How you feel inside when faced with certain things can determine how you'll reach your final destination.

– –

It's true that letting go is one of the hardest things to do because you have to settle with the past, engage in the present, and believe in the future. Doing all three things can be scary, frightening and strange, but once you start life will improve.

– –

It doesn't matter how many times you think you've failed. What's most important is that the number of times you get back up is higher! The more you get back up the more you succeed.

– –

Even though others may want to help you, sometimes you need to take the bull by the horns and just charge ahead on your own. Sometimes help from others may not be beneficial; it might be the easy way out, but not necessarily the best way. But only you will know this, so always listen to your instincts because at the end of the day, all you have is yourself to get you through.

– –

We've all been down hard and long roads before, but now you have the wisdom and the knowledge inside of you to create the best future for yourself. You just need to use it, and have the courage to make this year, your best one so far.

– –

When you start your journey along your spiritual path, you'll notice that most friends you had before will drop away, eventually leaving you alone. Take this time to get to know the real you, and once you have, you'll find that you attract new friends with the same interests and on a similar path as yours. Avoid asking yourself "why am I so lonely?" Instead, be grateful for the alone time and use it to truly get to know yourself.

– –

We are all born with the ability to change someone's life; we don't have to be professionals to help others. It's the intent within our hearts to want to help others, and that's how we can make a difference. Even those who are travelling down a path that is the opposite of our own, can help change others too.

– –

Sometimes we need to accept people and where they're at in their life. Understand you can't change them, as only they can do that. You can be there for them though, especially when they are ready to ask for your help. You can be the light in someone's life and teach them so they, hopefully, can be inspired to make a change for themselves.

– –

Stop concentrating on other people's thoughts and what they think of you. Instead, focus on your own thoughts and ensure they remain positive. Don't worry about negative comments; if you live by what other people think, you are not being true to yourself. Be the master of yourself and your own life.

– –

When life feels messy

Don't over-analyse or try to force things. Just follow your heart and not your head, for your head will lead you to the wrong places. When you follow your heart, your intuition comes from a place of love and love for yourself will lead you to magical places – all the right places.

– –

Don't let the past be the excuse for not succeeding in life. The reason we travel down bumpy roads is so we can learn what we agreed to learn, before arriving here on earth. We are here to learn so much. You can either let your lessons make or break you.

– –

You will find friends along the way who are compatible with your quirks, and you will join together to bring more love and light into this beautiful world. Remember to thank the Universe for bringing new friends who match your own quirkiness.

– –

Life

As soon as you set the intention to leave the past exactly where it is, the Universe will end the old and then bring you new opportunities and new joy into your life. Stop carrying it around with you, set it down, let it go and make way for the new.

– –

Having a rough day? That's okay – let yourself feel it. Just don't get lost in those feelings and thoughts. Instead, set the intention that tomorrow you will wake feeling wonderful, full of love and on top of the world. Don't be so hard on yourself.

– –

When life feels messy

It's time to release those negative thoughts out into the Universe, so your transformation can begin. Back away from the negative and focus on the love in your heart, and the gratitude you have for everything that you have right now, in this moment. What you put out will always come back; it's the Law of Attraction.

– –

Follow your passions, follow your heart and watch your dreams unfold before your very eyes. You have dreams, and when you start taking the steps towards them you will find that your life and you will be fulfilled in more ways than you have ever imagined.

– –

Life

We are all on our own paths in life, travelling at different speeds, and learning different things along the way. You have your own life to live at your own pace, so never compare yourself to anyone else. As long as you are coming from the heart, following your heart and giving love freely – and yes, even to those who have hurt you – then you are connecting to the divine source of life. To compare is to judge, not only others but yourself. Some of us have mountains to climb, deserts to cross, raging rivers to fight against, and meadows to dance through, but that does not mean anyone is better or worse; we are all equals. Live from the heart, and surrender all judgements to the one who created you.

– –

When life feels messy

Everyone has the power to make a difference. Don't let anything stop you from taking on the world and making a change. It only takes one person, just one person, you'll see.

– –

We tend to try and fit in with others to make ourselves feel better, to make ourselves feel important, but you don't necessarily need the approval of others to know your own worth. Feel what's right within as you travel through your journey. Feel and find your truth and your own worth. Get in touch with you, fall in love with yourself, and accept yourself wholly and completely.

– –

Life

Everyone has it, that feeling inside when you know that something feels right. It's called intuition. Trust it, trust it with all your heart and trust it with your mind; don't let that little nagging voice inside your head tell you otherwise. If it makes you feel good and giddy inside, then let go of that little voice that doubts it and trust yourself because you know more than you realise.

– –

When you find your true self, when you connect with your inner divine love, then you will come to understand what peace feels like. When you find your self, you are also able to help others along their journey in finding their true selves. It's okay to walk away from people who you no longer resonate with, and it's equally okay to walk the path alone for a while.

– –

When life feels messy

Only you can find your place in life; you are the change you seek. We can look to others for help and advice but it is up to you to take it on board. Find meaning in life, find something that you want and work towards it. What's the one dream that you've always wanted to create for yourself? Living life and being spiritual can be hard for some, but if you're putting all your effort into being spiritual then how are you going to live in the everyday world? While it's nice to stay with your head in the clouds, the reality is, that you are here on earth to live a human existence. You have been placed here to experience life. You can have a spiritual life and spiritual meaning, but you are here to live a human life too. The trick is to balance it all, balance your being human, and balance your spirit.

- -

Life

We often worry too much about the future and try to control events in our lives. But when you release and surrender all your worries, fears and control over to the Universe, you are blessed with the opportunity to relax, let go and have faith that all is unfolding exactly as it should be. Live life and enjoy it; when you release the reins you open your heart to that inner guidance of yours.

– –

Stop holding yourself back and just go for it. Life's too short to let your fears rule your life, so get out there and make the most of it. Enjoy each moment because you only live once.

– –

Everyone makes mistakes – sometimes more than once. The people who choose to go back to where they are because they haven't yet seen the light, are yet to step out of the darkness. Regardless of where they are, it's up to you to be an example – show them love and show them the way. We can either turn our backs on them, or help them find their way when they are ready to do so.

– –

Sometimes the best thing to do for your peace of mind is to get outside, breathe in that beautiful fresh air and thank Mother Nature for her wonderful gifts she bestows upon us. It really does soothe the mind and helps you see the bigger things in life.

– –

Life

Release all your worries and cares to the Universe and feel alive in this very present moment. Do something that makes you happy and makes you laugh. Let go of all the mind chatter and focus on enjoying now. Now is all you need at times to bring yourself back to the present. Not yesterday, not tomorrow, just now. Breathe.

– –

Even though at times you will feel alone, know that you are not alone in this world, reach out and find support in whatever way you can. There are others who are going through the same hurdles as you, and there are others who can help lift you up out of the darkness. There are angels among us everywhere and they don't necessarily have to have wings, just hold your head up and see, one glance is all it takes to see an angel.

– –

Blessings are everywhere; sometimes we may not find the answers to certain choices and sometimes we will, but everything is for us to go through so that we can awaken to our true spiritual self. Being spiritual is not about religion as such; being spiritual is about living your life with a heart of pure unconditional love and coming together as one.

– –

You can't search outside yourself to find happiness. Other people won't make you happy, situations won't find you peace, and money won't make you rich, as these are distractions and excuses to stop you from searching within. To truly heal yourself, you have to change the way you see your world. It all starts with you.

– –

Life

Be careful how you share your words. Words can heal or destroy others so before you talk, stop and think whether it will help or hinder someone's progress, then choose your words wisely.

– –

You will never find happiness if you keep searching for it. You have to slow your steps, calm your breathing and feel it from within; all your feelings and emotions come from within, and so too does your happiness.

– –

Don't forget to treat yourself to something nice every now and then. We give so much to others while we overlook giving to ourselves. You are important too and you deserve to give to yourself. When you give back to yourself you lift your spirits and in turn you lift the spirits of others. Make yourself a priority today; go on, you deserve it.

– –

You are responsible for your own life and for your own actions. How you choose to be responsible is up to you. You can choose to rise above it or you can choose to let it beat you.

– –

If you don't like where you are right now, know that you have the power to change the outcome. You are the SOUL writer of your story, and you can make the ending however you wish.

– –

Everything you need is right here, within YOU. You have the answers you are looking for; when you are silent enough you will hear the sweet nudges of the Universe. Stop for a moment and breathe. Now listen to your heart. Keep your dreams alive by always believing in the magic of the Universe. The Universe hears your every thought and feeling, so

Life

keep your thoughts and feelings high in vibration and the Universe will deliver.

– –

Sometimes you have to accept things for what they are and if you don't like it or if you can't change it, then it may be best if you walk away.

– –

Do you want to feel happy? Well you can; but first you have to decide if you want to feel happiness or sadness. Only you can make up your mind about this one. Find the blessings in your life and focus on them; really put all your heart and soul into being grateful for everything that's going on around you, and for the lessons that will make you stronger. Take a look around you and turn your thoughts up towards the heavens – scream out "I AM HAPPY!" Say it over and over again until you feel it with all your heart.

– –

When life feels messy

Let go of the past so that you can move forwards to a bright new future. Let go of your desired outcome for your future, so that you can live in the moment.

– –

There'll come a time in your life when things don't progress as you hope, and people will let you down. At this time, in your heart you know you'll have to let them go, so that you can grow. It will hurt, but it's the best thing that you can do to save yourself from prolonged heartache.

– –

Don't hold back; be your beautiful self, and let the world see who you really are.

– –

Being different and being real is something to be proud of, not to hide away from. So never be ashamed of shining your light, and of being who you really are. Step out of your hiding spot and show off the real you.

– –

Life

There will be many moments in your life where all you want to do is run away and hide. You mustn't, you must keep coming out of the shadows to face the very things that haunt you. Stay on your path of healing so that your hurts can be transformed into something wonderful. The road can be daunting and tiring, but it is the strength you gain, the wisdom you learn, the compassion and love you experience that makes it all worthwhile. Have your fits of rage, have your moments of sadness, have your moments of solitude but don't give up because in the end you will awaken to a new enlightened view of the world within you. You will eventually see that it was all brought to you for your higher purpose and always remember you are never alone.

- -

Take time to cultivate your own energy instead of relying on the energy of others to lift you up. It is inside you where you are able to build yourself up, and only you can proceed with this. Sure we can have others help us, but ultimately it is up to us. You want energy in certain areas of your life, then be willing to put it there. You can't wait for it to just happen; you have to do it yourself. Be the energy itself and you will see that life can take you on many beautiful journeys. Have confidence that you are all you need.

– –

Life is like school, where you learn so that you can become better, so that you can evolve on to the next stage, and excel in making this life a wonderful memory before you leave. Live in every moment, not attaching yourself to the outcomes, but instead letting every experience enrich you.

– –

No matter what is going on around you, take a little time every now and then to dream. When you give yourself the gift of dreaming, you take yourself to a world of endless possibilities. Dreams are your soul's way of connecting with you on your next step forward.

– –

When you climb to the top of a mountain, the view is magnificent; but remember to take in the journey along your way, because each moment, each obstacle and every lesson is important. It's what shapes your character for the future.

– –

There's no need to rush out into the world to make your mark. Slow down, persevere, take it step-by-step, make mistakes and learn lessons. Slowing down enables you to enjoy life's precious moments.

– –

When life feels messy

Save yourself by detaching from other people's dramas, before it's too late. When you get pulled into other people's trials, you end up taking on their energy and this can leave you feeling drained – both emotionally and physically. You have your own life to focus on, and if you're not strong enough you'll drown. Look at what's happening in your life and if there are dramas around you, then perhaps it's time to shield yourself before you drown.

– –

Free yourself and renew your mind, by changing the way you think to a way that sits well with your beliefs. Don't let others change the way you think and don't let them bully you into adopting their way of thinking. See the truth and find the truth within. It only takes one step at a time, to initiate changes in your life, so where are you going to start?

– –

Life

You can leave situations that are not right, but you can't run away from the pain or problems you hold within. Trying to forget about it will work for a little while, but in the end it will always come back until you deal with it once and for all. Instead of running from it, stand up and face your problems so that you can free yourself.

– –

Don't let others spoil your mind with their judgements. Instead, walk away and know that they aren't meant to be in your world. Send them love, and even a hug, but then let them be on their way.

– –

Let go of the old you, so the new you can emerge. Shine your light brightly so that others can see. Spread your wings and fly. Soar high and far into this brightly coloured, beautiful world that awaits.

– –

When life feels messy

Find the strength to pull yourself out of the rubble. Sometimes you can't rely on others for help and you have to do things for yourself. Don't wallow in self-pity of why these things happen to you; instead, rise above it and build something for yourself. These are lessons that you have to overcome.

– –

You deserve to be with someone who will really love you with all your faults and who won't bring you down. You deserve to be happy, with the right person, so don't waste your time or energy on someone who doesn't treat you the way you want to be treated. Love YOU first, and then go out and find someone to share your life with – someone who will love every single bit of you.

– –

Life

You can help heal the world by inspiring others with your wisdom. We all have wisdom inside, we just have to let go of the thoughts that tell us otherwise. Be like a phoenix and rise from the ashes.

– –

Sometimes you have to stop wishing for what could be, and accept where you are now. Go with the flow and let life take you on your journey.

– –

Your scars will not make you less loveable. To the right people, what you have been through will only make them love, appreciate and admire you more. The right people will admire you for all your strength, determination and the love you still hold for life.

– –

Sometimes, the more you try to see something, the harder it is to find. So close your eyes and take deep breaths. Listen to what your soul is telling you and feel the answers.

– –

When you forgive yourself and others, your healing can begin. When you let go of anger you let go of the internal struggle that you've held onto for so long. Release it and free yourself. There's no need to hold onto the pain any more. Once you let it go you can truly start living.

– –

Life

The "mistakes" we make are meant to teach us and if we don't learn the lesson we will go through the same scenario until the lessons are learned. It is up to you to wake up and realise that only you can change this. Stop putting yourself through the same thing over and over again; it's time to let go of the pattern and free yourself.

– –

Accept where you are in life and if you don't like it, get up and change it. You are the master of your own destiny and you hold the power to make things happen. But you are where you are for a reason, and only you will know this reason once you search within.

– –

Sometimes you need to let go of people who played a huge part in your life; especially if you keep finding yourself repeating the same mistakes with them. Stop and ask, "why am I doing this and what is the lesson here?" You have to put yourself first, and if they're dragging you down or if you're not getting anywhere with them, then it's better to free yourself from all the drama. Drama or freedom – it's your choice.

– –

In this day and age too many people are trying to be something they're not. Really, all we should be doing is being our authentic selves. When we start showing our truth, we attract more like-minded people. Like attracts like, just like fake attracts fake. Being real is better than being perfect or fake.

– –

Celebrate every day that you are alive, find joy in all the little things, dance through life as if no one's watching, believe that magic is happening all around you, feel gratitude with all your being, and praise each day you wake up. Life is too short to live with heaviness in your heart and negative thoughts, happiness is what makes you come alive. Find that happy place inside of you and live from there each day, be the joy you want to be.

– –

Whenever you see someone else in need, don't keep walking; instead stop and lend a helping hand or offer your ears for listening. Helping others helps you too because not only do you get to see someone feeling better but you will feel better within yourself for being able to help them.

– –

Trust that those repetitive thoughts you're hearing in your mind are the answers to those very questions you seek on your journey in life. If it feels right from the beginning through to the end, then these are the steps you need to take to propel you forward on your path. Never doubt those thoughts, trust your higher self, trust your angels and trust yourself that what you are hearing is correct. You are your higher wisdom, you have what it takes to listen, take a leap forward from your heart and into your truth.

– –

Above all things, choose peace and love. Choose kindness, compassion and forgiveness to heal others and yourself. See everyone with love, don't let other people's emotions affect yours, and know that you are worthy of great things. Always approach things from a place of love.

– –

Be a beacon of light and inspiration, to help others to see the light within themselves in the same way that you see the light in them.

− −

Don't hide yourself away from the world, come out and show yourself. You were made to stand out and be all you can be. You ARE a perfect creation made by God and you deserve everything the Universe wants to give you. Come out and let your beautiful self shine brightly.

− −

Surround yourself with people who make you feel great, lift you up and help you become your best self. Their belief in you will provide you with the self-confidence required to live a happy life.

− −

When life feels messy

Be what you want to be, do what you want to do, but stop making excuses about chasing your dreams. We are here on this earth to live life with no regrets, so take chances, and feel alive in the moment. Nothing is impossible. The word itself says "I'm possible." Everyone can create their dreams but first you have to step outside and go for it; stop waiting for them to come to you, because life just doesn't work that way.

– –

Everyone who enters your life is someone you can learn from. But first, you need to listen so you can see the lessons they are offering to teach us. People are sent to us to teach and help us learn, so be alert and aware so you can see the reason they've entered your life.

– –

Life

Reach out and offer someone an ear or a shoulder to cry on. It's not easy to ask for help when we need it most, so sometimes we need to reach out and make the first move.

– –

If an opportunity presents itself and changes your life for the better, don't question it. Just embrace it and watch the magic unfold.

– –

Take yesterday's lessons and use them today. How much the past defines you is completely up to you. Be the hero in your life; stand up for yourself and take action today to ensure a better tomorrow. Don't feel like you need to rewrite your story; instead, just continue on, but take the steps to make your life even more beautiful.

– –

Don't let someone else dictate how you live your life. When you let others tell you what to do, you are effectively giving away your power. It's not their life to live. If it doesn't feel right to you, then don't do it. Reclaim your power by speaking up with love, and by acting out through love. It is not up to others to decide how you live; it is entirely up to you.

– –

You can choose to be at peace with yourself, or you can choose to be at war with yourself. No one else and nothing else will bring you peace like you can.

– –

Life

Why do you regret the past? Why do you wish you were back where you were? You are here right now because it's where you're supposed to be. You can look back, and you can wish you were where you were a few years ago, or you can accept what has happened and move on from it. What you have been through has happened for your highest good. You are here to learn, you are here to evolve. No amount of dreaming of the past will get you back to where you were, so the best you can do is learn from it, forgive it and make your future the best that's yet to come. The future is in your hands and it's up to you to make an outstanding one.

– –

Learn to say "thank you" to the compliments, love, gifts and friendships that the Universe provides. We're all known for giving a little too much to those around us, and that's okay, so long as you let yourself receive too. Let the Universe give you what it wants, be receptive to change, and see how much more balanced you feel.

– –

When you feel out of balance or like your soul needs nurturing, then take time out. It's always beneficial to switch off from the rest of the world and take time to restore your balance.

– –

In life, it's okay to make mistakes because without them, how would we learn? Nothing in life is perfect so whenever you think you've made a mistake, don't beat yourself up about it. Instead, look at it as an opportunity to try again or to improve yourself or the situation. Mistakes are life's lessons thrown at us to help us right our wrongs, so praise yourself for what you are learning.

– –

Instead of over-analysing the opportunity before you, sometimes you just have to jump right in and say, "right, I AM going to do this." The more you question yourself, the more your negative thoughts creep in and you lose your chance. If it feels right and you want to do it, then go for it. What have you got to lose?

– –

Instead of over-thinking something, just speak up and ask. Over-thinking will bring you down and make you feel flat. So if you have something to say, just ask or talk about it. What's the worst that could happen? Even though it may not feel like it at the time, it's always better to know the truth, than to wonder and let yourself waste time on over-analysing.

– –

It doesn't matter what happened yesterday, yesterday is already gone and things have already been done. What matters is that you focus on the new day ahead. Bring love into your heart, along with peace in your mind that new beginnings lay ahead for you. If you didn't like yesterday, then let today be different for you.

– –

Life

Why do you worry so much? You are not on this earth to worry; you are here to live your life with happiness, peace and love in your heart. Release your cares and worries and you'll start to feel truly alive in every present moment.

– –

Try and BE in the moment; right now, right here, wherever you are. Just breathe and be. Don't think about tomorrow, don't think about yesterday, just think about right now. Be in the moment and learn to live in the now.

– –

Everything we go through in life happens for a reason. Even when times are at their toughest, trust that what you're going through is all for a higher good. Don't fight it, don't resist it, learn from it. Go with the flow and see what happens.

– –

When life feels messy

Every day we have opportunities to learn something new; but you must be open and aware of all that surrounds you at all times. Open your senses and you'll see that everything offers the chance for learning.

– –

There's nothing more important than forgiving yourself for past actions, hurts and sorrows. Doing so means loving yourself and moving on from past decisions and experiences. You deserve love and forgiveness no matter what has occurred in your past.

– –

Spend time in nature. Go for a walk or enjoy time in the garden with Mother Nature. She can diminish your worries and cares. Pause and listen with your heart. You never know what magical delights and discoveries you may hear from her.

– –

Life

Open your eyes like a child, and believe in other realms and the world's magical happenings. The more childlike your perspective, the more possibilities you'll be able to see. When you open your heart to innocent wonderment, you'll start to see what's really out there.

– –

If you're feeling stuck or blocked, go outside and breathe in some fresh air, to ignite your senses and reconnect with Mother Nature.

– –

The most powerful empowerment you can feel is to just BE YOU. There's no right or wrong here, there's only you. Don't be afraid or ashamed of who you are; you were made perfect and whole, and you still are.

– –

When life feels messy

Don't be afraid to ask the Universe for what you want. It may not give you everything, but you will get what you need. Drink from the Universe of life and be open to receive all that she gives you; you deserve happiness, love and a good life, so never be afraid to ask for it.

– –

You are a blessing in this world. Believe this with all your heart, because you are a wonderful, magnificent blessing. You are unique and completely amazing.

– –

Throughout your life, the Universe will bring you tests and lessons, and it's up to you to decide whether you let them consume you, or whether you can rise above and conquer them.

– –

Life

Free yourself from the pain and fear you hold inside. It's time to let it all go and start your life anew. Why do you drag yourself down so much, not only affecting yourself but your loved ones around you? Can't you see the pain that this causes you even more? Why do you hold on to so much anger and guilt from yesterday? Please see yourself as the light of God because this is what you are. Free yourself now and start healing immediately. When you let it all go you'll finally free yourself from the pain you hold inside. Be strong, be beautiful, be you, just be. When you stop looking back, you'll start moving forward.

– –

I believe in surrounding ourselves with people who lift us up, and who can help us to become our best selves. Their belief in you will lift you up and give you self-confidence to succeed in life; their beliefs and their words will help you recognise your own worth. If we didn't have friends to lift up us, where would we be?

– –

It's hard waiting for something when you want it so much, but if you let go of your worries and just be, what you want will come about much faster than you imagined.

– –

Sometimes you need to detach from all the drama and go live your own life, instead of trying to help others. If people aren't ready to listen to your advice, then there's not much you can do except be there to help them when they are ready. You have to step back and realise when you can't do it anymore. At which point, you need to release them so they can lead their own lives, learn their own lessons, and find their own path.

– –

You are the magic that's needed. All you have to do is look in the mirror and see your true self, to realise that you have the power to create magic in your life.

– –

Life is a constant learning journey. Embrace your lessons because they will create a bright future.

– –

When life feels messy

Yesterday's problems can impact your tomorrow, so let them go, look at what can be, and start a new beginning by learning how to live in the moment.

– –

We are all searching for something that will fill our life with meaning. What you have to realise is that YOU are the meaning. Stop searching outside and start looking within.

– –

Enjoy every step of the dance that is your life. Your steps don't need to be perfect, you just need to enjoy being in every moment.

– –

Life

Live in the moment. Don't let one negative thought in today; instead, make today positive and full of energy. Wake up and dance; dance on your toes with stars in your eyes and love in your heart – today is the day to LIVE!

– –

Let your radiant light shine bright. Be your beautiful self for all to see. You are amazing and deserve the best, so don't hide away from the world. Let the world see the real you. By being authentic, you are being true to yourself. Give the gift of you to the world.

– –

It may take a while to accept your past and everything that's happened, but once you do you'll see how it has brought you to where you are today. Make peace with it and let it go; now is the time to let new beginnings into your life.

– –

When life feels messy

Have you quietened your mind lately, so you can see what your life is really all about? Stop, listen and breathe. Take in your surroundings and see the beauty of life. There are so many things to learn and grow from; you just have to recognise them.

– –

Always live in your truth. If people don't like you for being you, then don't take that on board because that's their issue, not yours. When you live your truth, you'll attract more people who are living their truth because like attracts like.

– –

There are so many possibilities out there for you to experience. Just open your eyes and see all the magical mysteries surrounding you; it's all right there at your fingertips.

– –

Life

Just as a tree takes time to grow and blossom into its full self, so too will you. Slow down. There's no need to rush the natural order of your life.

– –

In the long-term, material items won't make you happy, nor will they bring you peace. Instead, to find this you must let go of all the external distractions and simply breathe, and be grateful for what you already have in your life.

– –

Do you ever feel like you're living your life inside prison walls? Break free from the chains that bind you. Get out and find the beauty in every day, release the past, and free yourself from the pains of yesterday. Life is too short to live within confinement, so live in this moment, and look forwards instead of backwards.

– –

When life feels messy

Be true to yourself and step out of the shadows that you hide behind. It's time to step away from your old way of life so you can become all that you can be in your world. There's so much to explore and see, but if you keep yourself locked away, you'll never get there.

– –

Why do you hold on so tightly to your past? Do you realise, you can free yourself any time, simply by letting go? Holding on will get you nowhere other than keeping you stuck behind your walls. Let them go and free yourself; when you stop being a slave to your past, you'll start becoming the master of your future.

– –

We can't be the controllers of everything in our lives; sometimes it's best to just let go of control and see what happens.

– –

Life

Whatever eventuates will be a blessing. Put energy into the things you can control: the way you think, feel, do and see things. Remember, only you control your outcome in life.

– –

Get out of your own way and start to see life as it should be seen: with love, beauty and awe.

– –

Don't put up barriers to the point that you stop letting people in. You can't do everything alone. Open your heart, let your guard down, and let in the people who want to help.

– –

Your life is precious and you have the power to make it your dream life. Giving up will never get you anywhere, but fighting for your life will take you further than you could ever imagine.

– –

Sometimes our wishes aren't coming to fruition because we focus too much on how we will get there, rather than trusting that you will get what you want in the end. Instead of focusing on the how, when and why, let go and trust in God, the Universe or whatever you believe in, and trust they will sort out the details for you.

– –

The path to success is often dark and filled with hardships, but understand that the destination will be worth it because in the end, all you will see is light. And once you discover the light, you'll find it hard to return to that place of darkness because the light will fill your soul, and open your senses to things that you've never seen before.

– –

Life

Do something different today by smiling at everyone you see. Smiling will lift their spirits, while also lifting yours. You never know, you might just make someone's day!

– –

If your world feels like it's crumbling around you, don't despair. The sun is still shining and there's still life left to live. Hold on to hope. Feel the fresh air and breathe it in. Let go of the life you've lived and start something new.

– –

Until you let go of your past you are never going to heal. To find peace, forgive yourself for all you've done to others, and forgive yourself for all you've done to yourself.

– –

Never underestimate yourself or sell yourself short, you are so much more capable than you think you are.

– –

When life feels messy

You are important in this world and you deserve to love yourself, as much as you give love to others. Start focusing on your inner-self, otherwise you will keep repeating the past, which will limit your growth.

– –

Money, clothes and cars will not buy happiness. Yes, it may bring you a little spark for a short while, but in the end that little spark will extinguish. Finding your inner-self will get you on the road to true happiness. Do not search for happiness in material things, because you will never be satisfied. Instead, search within and inside your heart you will always find happiness.

– –

Life

Stop chasing the wrong thing. Why do you keep avoiding all the important things in life, like YOU? Stop holding yourself back and find peace inside you now. Filling your life up with meaningless tasks will not get you the happiness you deserve. Can you see that? When you free your past, you will find healing. You can only be helped once you decide to start the journey yourself.

– –

I know life can get you down at times, but please remember you're the only one that has the power to turn your life around. Once you realise this, life can no longer tie you up or hold you down.

– –

You are responsible for the way you live your life. It is up to you how you choose to live it.

– –

It takes true strength to stand alone in the midst of darkness. True determination is shown by coming out and standing in the light. Be proud of yourself and all that you've achieved. There are brighter things out there for you.

– –

Everyone who enters our lives is someone we can learn from; but first we must learn to listen so we can recognise the lessons they need to teach us. God sends us people to teach and learn so be awake and aware, so you can see the reason they've entered your life.

– –

Life

Have you noticed that similar situations keep popping up in your life? This occurs when you haven't accepted your past doings; when you are still yet to learn the lesson. Recognise what keeps returning to your life; accept it, learn from it and then let it go. Until you truly release or resolve it, you won't be able to move on.

– –

Sometimes you have to release people from your life in order for you to fly. We can't change their minds or improve their lives if they are not willing to learn.

– –

New beginnings start from the smallest seed of hope. Always hold hope in your heart, belief in your thoughts, and live through each moment with magic in your eyes so you can watch your dreams unfold.

– –

When life feels messy

It's perfectly okay to take a step back from everyday life and give yourself some time out. It's actually one of the most important things you can do for yourself as it gives you time to breathe and reflect on life. When you feel that life is overwhelming, sit in silence and focus on your breathing. It's the easiest way to feel better.

– –

You are a perfect child of this Universe. You were created with pure love and you are still pure love. Learn to love yourself and to see yourself through the heart of God.

– –

Let the lessons you learn deliver you to your truth. Be brave enough and bold enough to step out of that darkness and into the light, and be the loving light that encourages others too.

– –

Your past can be a part of who you are. It can help you understand why things have happened, and provide awareness of why things continue to happen. It can make you more compassionate and forgiving, and bring you into alignment with what's best for you and your future.

– –

Forget the past hurts, pain and actions of what you may have done, or what others may have done to you. Leave it all in the past where it belongs, but never forget the lessons it taught you. Apply what you've learned so they are not repeated.

– –

Set your own safe and loving boundaries. Stand up for yourself, and always remember that you are in control of the way you react to others.

– –

Focus on you. Finding someone to fill an empty hole in your life is not the way to find happiness. Contentment and joy can be found within you. Let go of the need to find someone and instead, find yourself first. Enjoy your time alone and appreciate what you have around you. When you heal yourself and enjoy your life, and then the right person will come along.

– –

Live life to the fullest. Learn from every experience. Laugh everyday, enjoy life and of your experiences. Shine your light to the world, cry when you need to, give when you can, welcome all that you're given, and be the best you can be at all times. You only have one life to live so enjoy every moment.

– –

Life

Every new day is the chance to begin again; a second chance to change things, and create new beginnings. Don't put off waking up to life. Once you decide enough is enough, your life will begin to change in unimaginable ways. Take a chance and never look back. Create something new for yourself. You've got nothing to lose.

– –

Often, one of the hardest battles you'll ever have to fight is against yourself; the negative thoughts, the old ways of living. But once you start to find ways to heal yourself, you'll never look back. The greatest gift you can give yourself is freedom from your old life.

– –

Out of the ashes and into the new, a baby phoenix arises to begin life again. She takes all the lessons from the past, and turns them into wisdom for the future, teaching others all that she knows. While finding her purpose, she'll spread light and love to all. Standing tall in her power, softening at will, judging no one, she gives compassion and love to strangers. Rising to new challenges she knows what to do; she turns to God to heal. Rising from the ashes to give all she's got, this time she'll know what not to do.

— —

You don't need to spend hundreds of dollars to make yourself beautiful. Your true beauty lies within. When you fix yourself on the inside, you'll discover that your beauty has been shining all along.

— —

Life

Stand up, be strong and take back your power, and stop living in the past. Give yourself the gift of living in the moment, you deserve it.

– –

There is so much that the Universe wants to give you – even beyond what you might realise or feel like you deserve. Open your heart and let yourself heal from all past wounds. When you let love in, it will guide you so you can create the world you want to live in.

– –

Every day is a new chance to start over. Before you get out of bed think of five things you are grateful for. This will help the smile inside of you beam even more brightly, as you travel through your day.

– –

Be prepared to shine and radiate your love and magic to everyone you meet in your world. You are love, you are light, you are magic. Believe in yourself and all that you do. There is only one of you, so dare to be different and shine your light for all to see.

– –

Share your joy, your happiness, and your magic with everyone. Radiate these feelings of love to everyone who crosses your path because you never know who might be needing it. When you share yourself with others, you lift them up and in turn, you lift yourself up. There's no better feeling than being able to help others.

– –

You must step into the silence of your own heart to figure out where you are going and who you really are. You must reflect on all that life has given you, and all that life has taken from you and see what you have learned. Things always happen for a reason, and if we take the time to step outside of ourselves to gain some perspective from our situations, then we can analyse what and why it has happened. Everything is a learning curve and if we are not willing to learn or we if we are not conscious enough of our situation then how can we stop ourselves from repeating the same patterns? After heartbreak or failure, we must step into the silence of ourselves to gain what it is we thought we had lost. We must see what has been reflected back to us by others, after all it's not just the situations that we learn from but it is also the people that have been placed on our path that we can learn a great deal from too.

- -

When life feels messy

You are a gorgeous child of divine light; you are the beauty that speaks; you are love within. Never let anyone tell you different. You deserve all the goodness there is in the world.

– –

She reached for the light and took hold, not letting go for even a moment. She found that once the light enveloped her, she saw what she was missing all along. There inside the light she found herself; she awoke to what lay dormant through all the darkness she hid behind. The beauty, the love, the healing was what she was waiting for, and now she'd found it. She was home.

– –

Life

It's time to accept your responsibilities and own up to them. Stop making excuses and start doing what you need to do. This is your life and no one else's. Others may have played a role, but that's no reason to blame them or say "it's not my fault". Take action and stand up for yourself; be responsible, accept where you are, and then do something about it. Only you can do it.

– –

The sun is always shining in your world. But we sometimes miss it because we fill our minds with chatter and tasks and forget to take the time to see it and appreciate it for all it's worth.

– –

Everything we go through in life is an opportunity to learn, although not everyone realises this. It's up to you to be a positive influence in the lives of those people, to help show them the way.

– –

When life feels messy

Live in the moment, go with the flow, let life take you on a ride, and enjoy each day as it comes.

– –

Look inside your soul and listen to your heart and there within you will find your truth.

– –

You must put yourself first and foremost. You must find your strengths and recognise your weaknesses. You need to look deep within before you can help others on their journey.

– –

You are the one who makes the rules on how to live your life, not anyone else. You have the choice to give away your power to others, or to keep your power. No one else can make you do anything; it's up to you to make a stand in your life, and to seize what you want.

– –

Life

Decide once and for all that you are not going to be a slave to the past. You say it's so hard but in reality it is only hard if you allow it to be. Take the healing steps you need to help you on your path. The path you're on is there for you to learn the lessons of the past. When you find yourself repeating patterns stop, look back, recognise it, learn from it and then let healing begin. Until you do this you will not be able to move on.

– –

Surrender your past and all your pain; the strength to do so lies within. If you have the strength to hold onto it, you also have the strength and willpower to let it go. Freedom from the past is liberating, so give yourself the gift of freedom. Yes, sometimes it takes time to allow yourself to heal, but once you start on the path to self-healing it will get easier.

– –

You are not being selfish if you say "no"; you are protecting yourself from others, and if they don't understand that, then that is their problem, not yours.

– –

Life is not a competition. Each of us is travelling our own path in our own time, but yet we constantly compare ourselves to others. Stop placing labels and judgements on yourself because the road you travel is yours alone and it should therefore never be compared. Please be kind to yourself today, and remember we are all one; no one is better than you, and you are no better than others.

– –

Life

If you didn't like something that happened yesterday, then tomorrow morning, wipe the slate clean and start again. Let go of your cares and worries from the past, and say "hello" to a new day where your potential is limitless.

− −

She held on for so long. And freedom began from the moment she let go. When she let go, she felt all past pain and hurt wash away. And that was when her life truly opened up to all the magical possibilities around her. She started living the life she wanted, everything started to fall into place. Seeing the beauty she held within, she finally saw what she was made up of: pure love. She is finally free, she is peace and happiness; she is love.

− −

When life feels messy

Stick to your truth and do what feels right for you. Be willing to speak from your heart so that others can see and understand the passion and heartfelt emotion you put into your words. If boundaries are needed then state them with the intention of love. Others may not like your boundaries but by having them, you are showing others that you love yourself and that you are not willing to let them walk all over you. If they truly love you and want the best for you then they will also come from a place of love and understanding. After all, if boundaries are not placed, and if boundaries are not respected, then how else do we co-exist in this world? No matter where you are in this world, speak your truth and say what feels right for you.

--

Life

It's okay to grieve over your lost loved ones. Whether they are here on earth or have passed over to heaven, don't try to hold anything back, as these feelings will only resurface with more intensity if you try to keep it all in. Let it out, let your tears fall, let your heart break if it needs to because after the storm passes through your heart, there will always be a new horizon to stare at, a new beginning to start.

– –

When it all gets too much, and your head is filled with thoughts that confuse you, stop for a moment and reflect back on how it makes you feel. When you think with your heart and not with your head, then you will see the answers you are so longing for. We fill our mind up with constant thoughts of worry and fear that

we end up letting our mind run our life. Sometimes the mind doesn't matter; if the mind is filled with egocentric thoughts then you are not living from your heart's space. Take a step back, and ask yourself: "am I living from my heart or in my head?" "Is my mind filled with negative thoughts?" "Am I letting my mind rule my life?" Chances are if you are living in your head, you are not giving yourself a chance to live from the heart. Observe and be still in your heart. This can take much practise and perseverance, but the time and dedication you put into observing your thoughts and your heart can reap many benefits for your future. The mind will only serve to hold you back, whereas the heart can always move you forwards. Let your heart be your guide.

- -

Love

If only you could see that life is worth living and that you can have everything your heart desires. If only you could realise that fearful thoughts are but an illusion coming from the darkness in your mind. If only you could see that you are the miracle and change that you are waiting for. If only you could see the sun in your eyes, which also resides in your heart. If only you could step away from the prison of your mind, so life can show you a way to live from your heart. If only you could break down the barriers you have placed upon your heart, then you could let the light of love in. If only you could release the resentment and anger

Love

from your soul, then you would be free. You are such a beautiful soul and deserve so much in life, but your barriers hold you captive and you cannot see a way out. If only you could see that the Universe resides in you and not without you. You are so loved and this is the truth. You are the Universe, and I pray that one day soon, you see yourself the same way you are seen by those who love you.

– –

You were made with pure love, and inside you is pure love. Continue to shine your beautiful self so that you can be an inspiration to others, and help them to see the light within themselves. In turn, our world will shine and heal for the greatest good of all.

– –

When life feels messy

Learn to love each other no matter what the circumstances. Everyone is doing the best they can. Be kind, be compassionate, show forgiveness and send love to all you meet along the way, for everyone is going through their own battles.

– –

Open your heart and let yourself receive love. We all need love to keep going. Love heals pain from the past. Show love to yourself as you would to others – unconditionally. When you send love to those who've hurt you, it really does heal your heart. When you love freely, you'll attract and receive love in return.

– –

Remember the strength that resides in you, it'll get you through. Remind yourself that you are strong; you are love.

– –

Love

When you try and resist life and all that's flowing to you, a lot of energy is expended, which is why you feel so tired. Thoughts are just an illusion in your mind; it's what's in your heart that counts. Stop allowing your thoughts to rule the way you live. Allow yourself to open up to all the positives that you have, to all the possibilities that can happen. Allow yourself to accept what's being given to you, because when you allow yourself to accept, you give yourself the chance for change, the chance to look at things from a different perspective. If you're stuck on something, then ask for help. You are not alone in this world. Everyone has struggled through situations, and we are all here to help. Let your vulnerabilities be seen and heard because this is when you will find guidance from the purest forms and through the highest vibrations of love.

– –

Love is not the hardest thing to find, for it is already inside of you. When you are looking for it in outside sources, you are not giving yourself enough love. Be love, think love, embody love and you will never go another day without love. Love resides within. Love is all you need, and love will move you forwards in more ways than you can imagine. Seek love from others and you will never be nourished enough in life. You are the radiance and embodiment of love, so stop looking outside yourself and start feeling this within.

– –

You deserve love as much as everyone else. Too many times we forget to remind ourselves of this, and we end up putting everyone else first. Always remember that you are as important as everyone else.

– –

Love

It doesn't matter what's on the outside, it matters what's on the inside. Your heart beats out love, and that's all that matters. Your external appearance does not dictate who you are; it's the love that emanates from your soul that determines who you are.

– –

Love yourself for everything you've been through; there is no greater healing than love and forgiveness for yourself.

– –

Let the barriers down and let the light sprinkle some happiness upon you. Release your pain to the angels and open your heart to love once more.

– –

You are no better and no less than the person next to you. We are all equals. We are one. See yourself as love and feel the love around and within.

– –

Love was, love has, love does, and love is! Let the love of the Universe take you in her arms, let her fill your whole being and embrace you. Open your heart and arms to receive all that she wants to give, feel the warm embrace of the Universe guiding you and taking you along your path. Let go and flow with her. It's a wonderful feeling to be in the warm embrace of the Universe.

– –

Stop doubting yourself and follow your heart to where your dreams lie. You can do anything you want, yet you hide away thinking that you are worthless. You are more beautiful than you know. Give yourself the love you deserve and treat yourself with compassion and kindness.

– –

Love

Love is the answer when it comes to healing, so let love guide you in all the things you do. Always send out love to everyone; be love, think love, do love. Love brought you into the world and love will take you through your world. Feel other emotions, but always return to love.

– –

Wherever you go, go with love in your heart, let the love you have guide you. When you come from that pure place, you open your heart and mind to so much more. Give love to all, for with love there are no judgements. Love yourself unconditionally, when you start to love yourself for all your flaws then you bring forth more love to you. Love is unconditional and, therefore, healing.

– –

When life feels messy

Love is around you, no matter which way you go. We all experience relationships in our lifetime, and we all have our hearts broken at times, but that is no reason to ever give up on finding love. If you are looking for love, it will happen when you're truly ready, so for now enjoy being single and trust that love will find you when the time is right.

− −

In the midst of chaos, trauma, pain and sadness, you will always find love. Love will bring you out of the darkness and into your heart once more. Focus on love and the rest will start to fade away.

− −

You don't need someone to complete you all you need is love and joy in your heart because with this, you are already complete. Love is within you, you are love, and you are eternal.

− −

Love

Open your heart and let love in, let love guide you, let love heal you. Let go of anger, pain, fear and resentment and let love help move you forward. You deserve to move and grow in life, yet you hold on to the past, not letting yourself feel freedom. Release it and open your heart to the ever healing and guiding presence of the love you hold in your heart, the love that has been there all along. Surrender, set yourself free and feel the love.

– –

Let go of the blame, anger and negative emotions you feel towards others and decide here and now to send love to all those who may have wronged you in the past. By sending love you are giving yourself permission to heal from the past.

– –

Don't be a slave to the past any longer; instead let love in and heal for your future.

– –

The actions and words you said yesterday or today can have a profound effect on those around you, so use words and actions that reflect the love in your heart. What you did yesterday, or even months before, can have huge consequences if you are not careful. Choose love as the answer for yourself and others.

– –

Why do you try so hard to search for magic in other places and people you meet? Can't you see that you have all the magic you need inside of you? You won't find magic in the outside world until you see it within. You are gorgeous, you are light and you, yes YOU are the magic that you've been looking for all along.

– –

Love

Spread your love like wildfire. The more you give, the more you get, and the more you'll find peace within. Love has no boundaries; it is ever-expanding. It will heal our friends, families, enemies, and even strangers. Never be afraid to give out love. Hatred will hold you back, but love will move your world.

– –

Your love and compassion for others can set you free from your past. Love will guide you to new and wonderful beginnings; it will give you strength, and help make you see things that you never saw before. Open your heart and let love in.

– –

When life feels messy

Stop being so hard on yourself, you're doing the best you can at all times. See yourself with an open heart through the eyes of God; He made you perfect, He made you whole, and you are loved, and you are blessed. Be proud of yourself and how far you've come on this journey, because it's not about how far you've got to go, it's about all you've learned and achieved already. Love yourself for this achievement, because you are perfect exactly the way you are.

– –

Sometimes you have to listen to your wants and needs, and trust that your heart is telling you the right thing. It's never easy breaking someone else's heart but you have to do what's right for you. Release yourself from the guilt and pain of hurting them, and find peace in letting them go. This is your journey.

– –

Love

Open your heart and spread love. Be the light and love for others in their time of need. There's nothing like the feeling of love being directed at you, so give love whenever you can; it's the best gift you can give.

– –

Open your heart and mind to new possibilities, it's time to stop living with a closed heart and mind, there's so many wonderful things out there for you to explore, a new world is waiting for you, but first you have to soften your heart and let the magic of love in.

– –

Life is too precious to hold grudges towards loved ones. Make amends, settle your differences, see them for who they are and not for what they've done. Love unconditionally, because at any moment they could be taken from you.

– –

When life feels messy

When you focus on love, so many things expand and change within. You open up your channels for creative expressions, you open up your mind for positive thinking; there are so many possibilities when we focus on love. Love is all you need.

– –

Love is in the air. See it, feel it, breathe it. Let it light your heart and guide you everyday in everything you do. Love will make you happy and move you forward. Live your life with pure unconditional love for all.

– –

You are worth saving; you are worth fighting for. Never give up on yourself. The road to self-discovery may be very confronting at times, but once you fight through those emotions and truths, you will find what you're looking for. Peace, happiness and love all lie within, and they are worth fighting for.

– –

Love

Fall in love with yourself, get to know the real you before falling in love with anyone else. Find out all the things that make YOU smile, that bring YOU joy. Follow your path of self-bliss. It can be hard on this journey when we meet many others along the way because sometimes their likes and dislikes and their truths may merge with our energy, that's why it's important to take regular time outs to get to know the real you.

– –

Never forget that you are as important as others. If you feel out of balance or drained, give yourself some time away from others. To be able to help others is a beautiful gift, but you have to look after yourself too. It's all about achieving a balance between giving and receiving. Love yourself because you are worth the time and energy.

– –

Let light in. Let love in. Let it be the reason for getting out of bed every morning. Forgive yourself and forgive others. Now is the time to let go of the darkness that you've held onto for so long. There's so much to explore in life, but you first need to let go of all the pain and let true love into your heart. Love heals everything.

– –

Never doubt that you are amazing. No matter what your past or present, you are worthy of love.

– –

See others through the eyes of love. Show compassion to everyone you meet. Do not judge the behaviours of others, for they may be travelling a rocky road. Everyone has been through hard times, and just because they act or lead their lives differently, it does not mean they deserve to be loved any less.

– –

Positivity

When life feels messy

Never let the fear of failure stop you from achieving your dreams. When you let fear in, it can become overwhelming to the point of paralysing your progress. Your thoughts create your life, so try and keep your thoughts positive. Like attracts like, so by thinking positively, more positive things will come your way.

– –

Can you see how your thoughts directly create your world? If you are focused on the negative, then try to add in one positive thought per day, and before long you will start to see your world in a new, positive light.

– –

Positivity

If you are drowning in your sorrows, then you are choosing to make life worse for yourself, by choosing to stay immersed in your past. But once you learn how to swim away from your sorrows, you will never drown in them again.

– –

Life is for living, so embrace change and seize life. Feel the love in the air, take life as it comes, let go of negative thoughts, take chances, look in the mirror and tell yourself you're worth it, never look back, say "I love you", love yourself, dance in the rain, smile at everyone, run, skip and hop, hug a tree, jump in puddles, make angels in the snow.

– –

When life feels messy

Stop feeling sorry for yourself. Let go of the negative thinking and stop playing the victim. Yes, things went wrong in the past and yes it hurt, but it happened for a reason. Let that reason be a blessing and not a hindrance in your life.

– –

The light in you is always shining, you just have to open up your heart and believe that anything is possible. In the midst of darkness there is always a glimmer of hope. You just need to reach in and pull it out.

– –

Laughing lifts you up and makes you feel good. If you laugh every single day, you'll live a happy life.

– –

Positivity

The role of your ego is to feed on negative thoughts. That's why it's often hard to listen to yourself when your ego is in the way. The only way to quieten your ego is to conquer the negative thoughts by doing what you think is hard or impossible.

– –

You need to stop being so hard on yourself, and start realising that you are doing the best you can. The harder you are on yourself, the harder it is to climb out of that black hole you're in. You are worth more than you think you are. You are love, light and everything beautiful in between; believing in yourself brings out the best in you.

– –

When life feels messy

Your happiness is directly impacted by your thoughts about yourself. No matter how much you try and get approval from others in your life, you can't be truly happy until you start realising that it all begins with what you believe about yourself. You are magic. You are brilliant. You are perfect, exactly the way you are. Believe this with all your heart.

– –

Today is a new day and a new chance to change your thoughts to focus on what you want to attract, instead of what you don't want to attract. Think positive, feel positive, be positive; and your desires will come to fruition.

– –

Positivity

Stay positive, no matter what comes your way. Even when it feels like there's no hope and you want to give up, hold on tight to hope and faith and never let go.

– –

You have what it takes to make life worth living, so never give up on yourself. You are gorgeous and no one can ever take your beauty away from you. Believe in you and all your dreams; you're worth it.

– –

You're doing the best you can, please don't strive to be perfect, as there is no such thing. Just keep going, do the best you can and remain true to you. You are one of a kind, you are unique, you were born to be different and to stand out; so shine your light for all it's worth. You deserve to shine.

– –

When life feels messy

If people do not respond positively to you then let them go so they can live their own life. Ask your angels to bring the right people into your life, and they will deliver.

– –

You have so much to be thankful for, so celebrate every day of your life. You only have one life, so let your hair down; play and dance like a child, and most of all, enjoy every moment.

– –

You create what you send out into the Universe, so always try and keep your thoughts positive. Think happy, think love, think positive, and it will all be returned to you. Likewise, if you think negative, think anger, or think sadness, then that too will be sent your way. Maintain positive thoughts and you will change your life for the better.

– –

Positivity

Try to keep your thoughts positive and ask the Universe to help you with whatever you are going through. By staying positive will you attract more positive into your life; conversely, negative thoughts will only pull you down.

– –

Let go of people who weigh you down and hold you back. Let yourself fly free from the negative people in your life. You deserve to be surrounded by those who lift you up and inspire you and move you forward. There's nothing better than the beautiful feeling of being surrounded by positive people in your life.

– –

When life feels messy

Look for the positive in every situation, because the negative will only weigh you down. There is always something positive happening in your life even if it isn't to do with that particular situation. Focus on the good and the positive in your life, and more positive will enter your life. See positive, feel positive, be positive.

– –

When you surround yourself with people who believe in you, your energy will lift and empower you to a higher level. But when you surround yourself with people who bring you down, who are closed to change, you can get sucked in and pulled under. Surround yourself with positive people so you can keep moving forwards.

– –

Be mindful of what you think – the mind is very powerful and effective at manifesting what you focus on.

– –

Positivity

Let go of those negative thoughts that you keep obsessing over, and replace them with positive, uplifting thoughts. The more you think about them the more "mind chatter" you'll create. You have the power to choose the thoughts and situations you want in your life, so create positive ones today.

– –

No matter how much you've been broken, you still have strength to fly.

– –

Make a change and affirm your positive thoughts and feelings, so that the challenges put before you do not overwhelm you.

– –

When you focus on your fears you attract them, so let go of the fears and worries, and focus on the positive.

– –

When life feels messy

It's time to get out there and beat the situation you find yourself in. Stop feeling sorry for yourself and stop doing nothing. You can do something to improve your perception of the situation.

– –

Give your dreams the energy they deserve. Don't let fears take up time and space in your mind because when you hold onto fears you'll create more. Instead, focus on your dreams and the steps you need to take, to make them come alive.

– –

If things seem hard right now, don't let it bring you down even further, instead take yourself outside and marvel at all the beauty that the Universe bestows on you; the trees, the stars, the birds, the moon, the bright blue sky and clouds. There's so much more to see and feel than your problems. Taking a break and heading outside will do wonders for your soul.

– –

Positivity

Always keep your thoughts about your future positive, because the moment you give up on your dreams or visions of your future, you'll stop attracting it into your life. When you take yourself away from the positive manifestations of hope and belief, the Universe will stop working for you and you'll start to bring yourself down with negative thoughts.

– –

Yes, it takes dedication and perseverance to achieve something you really really want, but equally important is staying positive until you get it. You can't have a positive future if you don't believe in it, can you? Try and break free of negative thoughts and beliefs, and never ever give up on yourself.

– –

When life feels messy

Keep your words, thoughts and actions positive and inspirational in everything you do and with everyone you meet. You never know you may just be helping out someone in need by shining your gorgeous beautiful light.

– –

The more you keep feeding a problem, the more energy you give it, making it worse until you let it bring you down to a point where you can't focus on anything but that problem. Instead, let thoughts shift and refocus on the good in your life. Take yourself away and step out in nature; re-centre yourself to be in the present. Realign yourself and realise how wonderful and beautiful your life is. Taking a break and stepping back from it will help you to avoid the fall.

– –

Positivity

You have to keep your thoughts positive at all times because the moment you let one negative thought creep in, it can be hard to climb back out of the darkness. Ego likes to creep in and take over, so don't let ego win. Ego is darkness, and will feed you negative thoughts. Find the light and hold on to it, as it will be the only thing that sets you free.

– –

It takes practise to be aware of your thoughts, but if you keep sticking with it, you will find that your thoughts become more positive everyday. Don't give up on yourself. You deserve to have a wonderful life filled with beautiful thoughts and you will; just keep persevering and you will soon start to see results of your life changing for the better.

– –

When life feels messy

Sometimes you have to temporarily focus on your fears in order to do whatever it takes to overcome them. By focusing on them, you will see inside yourself and how you have the power to overcome them. Don't let the negative thoughts in your mind take over, instead take over your negative thoughts and tell yourself that you can do anything you set your mind to; replace those thoughts with positive affirmations.

– –

Whatever you think about comes about, so keep your thoughts positive and your eye on the end result. Thinking positive will help make your manifestations come to fruition much faster than you ever thought possible.

– –

Positivity

When life feels like it's getting on top of you, take time out and get yourself outside to reconnect with the divine energies of the earth; a little grounding can go a long way. Don't be so hard on yourself for letting things get on top of you, after all, you're only human, and you have a right to fall down, as long as you get yourself back up again. Resist the urge to stay down, and embrace the magical qualities of life once more.

– –

Don't be so hard on yourself, there's nothing worse than feeding yourself negative thoughts. The more you are hard on yourself the harder it is to push through it, just tell yourself that all will be well, and try again the next day. After all, every day is new day, a chance to start over, wipe the slate clean from the day before and resolve to begin again with a brand new day and a brand new set of positive thoughts.

www.ingramcontent.com/pod-product-compliance
Lightning Source LLC
Chambersburg PA
CBHW070545010526
44118CB00012B/1228